WOMEN IN SOCIETY A Feminist List edited by Jo Campling

The 1970s and 1980s have seen an explosion of publishing by, about and for women. This new list is designed to make a particular contribution to this process by commissioning and publishing books which consolidate and advance feminist research and debate in key areas in a form suitable for students, academics and researchers but also accessible to a broader general readership.

As far as possible books will adopt an international perspective incorporating comparative material from a range of countries where this is illuminating. Above all they will be interdisciplinary, aiming to put women's studies and feminist discussion firmly on the agenda in subject-areas as disparate as law, physical education, art and social policy.

WOMEN IN SOCIETY
A Feminist List edited by
Jo Campling

Published

Sheila Allen and Carol Wolkowitz   **Homeworking: myths and realities**
Jenny Beale   **Women in Ireland: voices of change**
Angela Coyle and Jane Skinner   **Women and Work: positive action for change**
Gillian Dalley   **Ideologies of Caring: rethinking community and collectivism**
Leonore Davidoff and Belinda Westover (*editors*)   **Our Work, Our Lives, Our Words: women's history and women's work**
Emily Driver and Audrey Droisen (*editors*)   **Child Sexual Abuse: a feminist reader**
Diana Gittins   **The Family in Question: changing households and familiar ideologies**
Frances Heidensohn   **Women and Crime**
Ursula King   **Women and Spirituality: voices of protest and promise**
Muthoni Likimani (*Introductory Essay by Jean O'Barr*)   **Passbook Number F.47927: women and Mau Mau in Kenya**
Jo Little, Linda Peake and Pat Richardson (*editors*)   **Women in Cities: gender and the urban environment**
Sharon Macdonald, Pat Holden and Shirley Ardener (*editors*)   **Images of Women in Peace and War: cross-cultural and historical perspectives**
Shelley Pennington and Belinda Westover   **A Hidden Workforce: homeworkers in England, 1850–1985**
Vicky Randall   **Women and Politics: an international perspective** (2nd edn)
Rosemary Ridd and Helen Callaway (*editors*)   **Caught Up in Conflict: women's responses to political strife**
Patricia Spallone   **Beyond Conception: the new politics of reproduction**
Taking Liberties Collective   **Learning the Hard Way: women's oppression and men's education**
Clare Ungerson (*editor*)   **Women and Social Policy: a reader**

Forthcoming

Eileen Aird and Judy Lown   **Education for Autonomy: processes of change in women's education**
Niam Baker   **Happily Ever After? Women's fiction in post-war Britain**
Jennifer Breen   **Women and Fiction**
Maria Brenton   **Women and Old Age**
Joan Busfield   **Women and Mental Health**
Ruth Carter and Gill Kirkup   **Women in Engineering**
Lesley Ferris   **Acting Women: images of women in theatre**
Tuula Gordon   **Feminist Mothers**
Frances Gray   **Women and Laughter**
Eileen Green, Diana Woodward and Sandra Hebron   **Women's Leisure, What Leisure?**
Jennifer Hargreaves   **Women and Sport**
Annie Hudson   **Troublesome Girls: adolescence, femininity and the state**
Susan Lonsdale   **Women and Disability**
Mavis Maclean   **Surviving Divorce: women's resources after separation**
Jan Pahl   **Marriage and Money**
Lesley Rimmer   **Women's Family Lives: changes and choices**
Susan Sellers   **Language and Sexual Difference: feminist writing in France**
Jane Thompson   **Introducing Women's Studies**
Deborah Valenze   **The Other Victorian Women**
Janet Wolff   **The Art of Women**
Ann Woodhouse   **Sex, Gender and Transvestism**

A Hidden Workforce

Homeworkers in England, 1850–1985

Shelley Pennington
and
Belinda Westover

**MACMILLAN
EDUCATION**

First published 1989

Published by
MACMILLAN EDUCATION LTD
Houndmills, Basingstoke, Hampshire RG21 2XS
and London
Companies and representatives
throughout the world

Distributed in the U.S.A. by New York University Press.

Printed in China

British Library Cataloguing in Publication Data
Pennington, Shelley
A hidden workforce: homeworkers in
England, 1850–1985.—(Women in society)
1. England. Women. Home employment, 1850–
1985
I. Title   II. Westover, Belinda, *1949–*
III. Series
331.4
ISBN 0–333–43296–7 (hardcover)
ISBN 0–333–43297–5 (paperback)

Series Standing Order

If you would like to receive future titles in this series as they are published,
you can make use of our standing order facility. To place a standing order
please contact you bookseller or, in case of difficulty, write to us at the address
below with your name and address and the name of the series. Please state
with which title you wish to begin you standing order. (If you live outside the
United Kingdom we may not have the rights for your area, in which case we
will forward your order to the publisher concerned.)

Customer Services Department, Macmillan Distribution Ltd,
Houndmills, Basingstoke, Hampshire, RG21 2XS, England.

To our mothers

Contents

List of illustrations

Preface

Homeworkers are most often women who work in their own homes for an outside employer. They are paid on a piece-work basis. In general they work alone but they are sometimes helped by members of the family, neighbours or friends. The work is usually unskilled and of a boring and repetitive nature. The economic status of the homeworker, stemming from her structural position in the economy, has little or nothing in common with the independent craftsman working in his own home before the onset of industrialisation. Homeworkers work without supervision and the employer passes judgement only on the finished product. They have no real contact with the economic sphere, generally meeting the employer or the sub-contractor only when collecting or returning work.

This volume is an analysis of the economic and social position of the predominantly female labour force of the homework industries from 1850 to 1985. We have set the discussion of homeworkers in the context of the changing socio-economic status of women during this period. The type of work women have been able to do and the wages they could and can expect are constrained not only by material factors but also by the prevailing ideology. The nineteenth-century view that a 'woman's place is in the home' meant that women who wished to work, or more often those who *had* to work, were extremely limited in their choice of employment. This situation has continued through the twentieth century to the present day.

One way that married women could earn money and not contradict the assumptions about their domestic role was to take in homework. A study of homework illustrates the fallacy of the belief that the working class has ever existed on a family wage earned by the male breadwinner. The Industrial Revolution transformed the work of women and created the division between home and work. This meant that problems of childcare and domestic responsibilities arose when married women tried to engage in paid employment outside the home. Many of them had to make ends meet by taking in lodgers, housecleaning for others, charring, child-minding or taking in homework.

The homework labour force was recruited from a cross-section of the female population. Lower-middle-class girls did homework as a repectable way of earning money before marriage, and many continued this as a clandestine occupation after marriage. In the countryside large numbers of single and married women worked in the rural home industries, and in the urban centres married women, unmarried mothers, single parents and widows might all take in homework at some time in their lives. Today, the composition of the homework labour force is slightly different but many of the reasons for choosing homework remain unchanged. Women need to earn money and yet are often confined to the home by domestic commitments.

This book looks at the composition of the homework labour force throughout our period and also at the alternatives open to women and how these have changed. The industries employing home-workers in the period 1850–1914 were many and varied, and were distributed all over the country. We take a detailed look at the work processes involved in some of the most important of these industries, for example glove-, boot- and shoe-making, lacemaking, straw plaiting and sack making. The tailoring industry, which was one of the largest employers of homeworkers, is discussed in detail. There have been some attempts over the years to improve the situation of homeworkers either by organising them into unions or by legislation and we critically evaluate these attempts. After the widespread concern about homeworking in the early twentieth century, it almost appeared as if homework had died out and very little was heard about it in the inter-war or post-Second World War periods. There was a revival of interest in homework in the mid-1970s and researchers found that very little had changed for this 'hidden workforce'. Relatively little has been written about homeworkers, and material relating to this group of workers is sparse. Documentary material has been supplemented in this work by the use of oral evidence from women who were themselves homeworkers. In this way, it was possible to get some idea of how

women fitted in their waged work with their unpaid domestic
responsibilities.

SHELLEY PENNINGTON
BELINDA WESTOVER

1

A woman's place is in the home

In pre-industrial society the father ruled over the family. However, women had a definite work role within the family, and hence also in society. Women's moral inferiority may well have been widely acknowledged but they were seen as physically capable of hard work. All members of the family helped to produce their means of subsistence. In working-class families the Industrial Revolution brought a decline in the fathers' control along with the possibility of a life outside the family for women. This brought a kind of 'freedom' for working-class women but in so doing it deprived them of a definite work role and status, enforcing a new kind of dependency which made it necessary for them to sell their labour power outside the family.

A rigid separation developed throughout society: life was divided into public and private spheres. Society was transformed from one organised around household production to one organised around large-scale factory production and governed by the dictates of the Market. Women were deprived of their traditional productive skills in textile manufacture and food processing as these were transferred out of the household unit into the factory system. These developments deprived women of their dignity and status and created the conditions in which the 'woman question' could develop. Before the Industrial Revolution women had clearly defined economic and social roles, and it was only after industrialisation that questions arose concerning what work should be deemed right and suitable for women. Should women work outside the home? Should women work for wages? Conditions stemming from the Industrial Revolution made the sexual division of labour into a controversial issue.

A distinct middle-class consciousness developed as a result of these economic changes. Increased productivity meant increased wealth and there was no longer any need for the whole family of these strata of society to engage in productive work. Economic changes had direct implications for the roles and structuring of the family. A man's status became dependent upon his wife not going out to work. The essentially Victorian and middle-class ideal of womanhood stood for the sanctity of the family, for the status quo and a form of political stablility. A threat to the family was seen as a threat to the very fabric of society itself.

Protestant evangelicalism was a crucial influence in the formation of the ideology of domesticity. The moral and social conservatism of the evangelicals evolved a religion that was compatible with economic competitiveness. Middle-class evangelicalism was concerned with the creation of a new morality. It was a movement to moralise society itself, to inject into in a new code of respectability. Central to the creation of this new morality was a redefinition of the woman's position within the family. Evangelicals saw a need to engage in constant struggle against sin; the household was a haven and the major institution from which this battle could be waged. The middle-class family was to provide a model to aspire to: women were to be at the very core of this family and they were to be responsible, by example, for the moral regeneration of the nation.

For a woman to exert this influence, she had to remain in the home as much as possible. Her daily domestic existence had to be an example of moral excellence. In this way, patriarchal authority sought justification in religion itself. Evangelicalism in the form of domestic ideology was an appeal to a morality which stressed the religious importance of motherhood and the sanctity of the home. The ideology of feminine domesticity played the part of a social control mechanism that sharply curtailed women's sphere of action. Its strength lay in its appeal to morality and its stress on the importance of motherhood, the family and home life.

Although an unrealistic goal for many, the new model of domesticity and femininity proved a tenacious ideal. It was helped by the publication of large numbers of manuals and etiquette books which stressed marital submission and passivity. However, women of the middle class had little in common with their working-class sisters. The majority of the middle class assumed that working-class women would need to work. This work, however, was expected to coincide with women's natural sphere – domestic service was seen as the ideal employment for single working-class females. So, whereas middle-class women were not to experience productive work at all, the working-class woman's employment was seen to end with marriage.

In many instances the agrarian and industrial revolutions destroyed women's opportunity to engage in productive work by ending the existence of the individual/household as the basic economic unit. Furthermore, they provided the opportunity to create wage differences based on gender that allowed women to engage in productive work only in the lowest-paid sectors of the economy. As a consequence of these two factors, married women became economically dependent upon their husbands. The single woman gained a degree of independence in that she retained control of her wages as the individual wage replaced the family wage. In practice, however, her restricted choice in the employment field and the extremely low wages paid to women meant this was a very limited independence.

As the middle class emerged as the dynamic class, exerting its influence in economic, cultural and political spheres, institutions were reshaped to meet specifically middle-class ends and ideals, and the social institution in which the middle class made itself supreme was the family. New and revised roles were assigned to its members in keeping with the middle class's social and moral philosophy. At the heart of the family ideology was the belief that the male breadwinner went out to work to maintain his wife and children as dependants in the home. This concept of the 'family wage' was one dependent upon a rigid sexual division of labour. Men went into the labour market and women were contained in the home. It was an ideology which assumed that the husband was not only able but also willing to support his wife and children, and the economically unproductive wife was at the core of this ideology.

The ideal of the family wage and its influence on women's roles and status in the household is crucial to an understanding of women's position in the work-force. Low wages kept women dependent on men and encouraged them to marry. Married women were likely to perform domestic tasks for men. In this way men benefited both from higher wages and from the domestic division of labour.[1] The ideology of domesticity meant that the working man was cushioned by women who provided the essential services of food, clothing and childcare.

Authority in the home, which was increasingly held to be a private domain, could also compensate men for the loss of autonomy many experienced in the workplace. The earner of the family wage, the male breadwinner, was entitled to certain privileges within the household. The allocation of housekeeping and pocket money was often in the hands of men. As the main, or only, wage earner, the man could claim the lion's share of the food, especially meat, at mealtimes. He usually had money he could spend on himself and he had access to medical care. Women, on the other hand, made do with an inferior diet, such as bread, they received poor medical attention even in childbirth, and seldom had money to spend on themselves.[2]

In practice many married men simply did not earn enough to support a wife and children, and the family wage was an ideal rather than a reality. The ideal made it increasingly difficult for the wives, and sometimes also the daughters, of skilled workmen with aspirations to respectability to be seen as wage earners. They were compelled to earn as much as they could in casual, ill-paid jobs like charring, taking in lodgers, childminding and homework. These activities were seen as both practical and acceptable extensions of their normal tasks. The double responsibility of domestic work and paid work meant that it was difficult in any case for married women to take full-time jobs.

Because it was assumed that married women were being financially supported by the family wage earned by their husbands, their earnings were described as 'pin money' by employers, by the press and by government bodies. The term 'pin money' is sometimes used to mean money earned by a married woman to buy luxuries for herself or her family, but it can also be used to mean *any* money earned by married women regardless of the needs of the family. The whole notion of 'pin money' is problematic since it calls into question ideas of what constitutes luxuries. In practice, the idea of 'pin money' was used to justify the low wages of women workers. It was assumed that they were working not from necessity but to fill in time or to buy luxuries. The employer could congratulate himself that he was not tempting women out of their traditional sphere with the offer of high wages.

The idea of family wage meant that there was a constant reserve of cheap, unskilled, non-militant labour in the form of married women. Employers could in certain instances make use of this to undercut male labour and weaken the bargaining position of the trade unions. The persistence of the view that women's wages merely supplemented a male wage served to weaken the bargaining position of both males and females in the economy. The fear that women would undercut male wages meant that male and female trade unions often failed to work together. The family wage therefore helped to weaken working-class unity and militancy by creating conditions for conflict.

The family wage and its underlying concept of dependency meant that no recognition was given to married women's domestic or economic contribution to the family. Domestic work was not acknowledged as 'real work'. The idea of the family wage has disguised the fact that the working-class woman's contribution to the family income has been an essential one. This volume, in describing one very important and hidden area of women's employment, will go some way towards illustrating the fallacy of the belief that the working class has been supported and reproduced on the basis of the family wage.

The model of the male breadwinner and the dependent wife began to filter through the various strata of the working class during the nineteenth century. The first aim for this ideal were the respectable working class, but the question of how this dominant stereotype became accepted by the working class is not an easy one to answer. No doubt one important source for the literate was its portrayal of the ideal through the increasing amount of literature and magazines aimed at the respectable working class and through a number of middle-class novels, such as those of Charles Dickens, which were read by this sector of the population. Domestic service was also the largest employer of female labour and it may well have been the case that working-class girls absorbed some of the middle-class values they saw in practise during this period of their lives and attempted to attain some approximation to this in their own families.

One form of direct intervention was the policy of many employers who refused to take on married women or allow them to continue in employment. It was believed that married women's employment would lead to sexual promiscuity and an inability to carry out adequately her duties as a wife and mother. The working-class males's reluctance to allow his wife to work outside the home was not just an embracing of middle-class values. His hesitancy and suspicion can be traced back to the early days of industrialisation.[3] Women's work outside the home had been seen then, as later, as a threat to his status as chief breadwinner in the family. This hostility was only ever really overcome in specific areas, such as the textile regions that had a certain unique culture and tradition of women's work. The working class's unwillingness to accept married women's work outside the home is reflected in the treatment of women by the male trade union movement. Many unions were reluctant to accept women members while others even conducted strikes against women workers. A certain element of this middle-class model of domesticity, albeit in a different form, was therefore already latent within the working-class itself.

There were also other ways in which the image of what women were supposed to be and to do was transmitted to working-class girls. One of the most pervasive was the education system which had started to expand in the 1860s. The type of education girls received in the late nineteenth century sought to prepare them for their future role as wives and mothers. Domestic subjects, including needlework, became compulsory for girls. Girls were being trained for jobs in domestic service or in dressmaking, millinery or tailoring – the only alternatives open to working-class girls in most areas of the country at that time.

The last quarter of the nineteenth century saw an increasing dependence by children on their parents. Compulsory elementary education coupled with the Factory Acts, which reduced the hours which children could work and the age at which they could start work, meant that children became an economic liability rather than an asset. School hours and school holidays meant that married woman were restricted in the hours that they could work.

The view that marriage was the primary goal for women and that once married, women were supported socially, politically and financially was enshrined in the law in the nineteenth century. Until the Married Women's Property Act of 1884, married women had no right to own property. What was her property before marriage became her husbands afterwards, and he could dispose of it as he liked whether they lived together or not. Until the passing of the Act, money earned by a married woman also belonged to her husband. Legal custody of children belonged to the father until the 1870s when mothers gained some limited power over children up to the age of seven. Married women could not sue or be sued for contracts, nor could they enter into contracts except as agents of their husbands. Although the law had by the beginning of the twentieth century modified the position of married women, the view that wives were the property of their husbands lingered on. The idea that married women of all classes were (or should be) the financial dependants of their husbands had important effects on women's employment position and on their standard of living.

Women were among the poorest of the population in this period. They lived longer, so that poor women were more likely to be widowed with young children to support, and women were more likely to survive past work into old age and poverty. Women were less likely than men to remarry if widowed or if the marriage broke up and even less so if they were caring for young children or dependent relatives. Women's work opportunities were more limited than men's and they could only earn between a third and a half of the male manual workers' wages at any time before 1914. Many wives were left alone because of desertion or the temporary absence of the husband. Moreover a high proportion of Victorian women remained single, and even within a two-parent family, wives might experience lower living standards than their husbands. Poor women had more deficient diets and suffered worse health than men and this was exacerbated by continual childbearing. Low pay made saving for health and other care difficult, and women were generally excluded from mutual savings institutions like Friendly Societies through which working men could protect themselves against sickness and old age. Women were reduced to support from charity or the Poor Law, or help from family and neighbours. The prevailing belief that the man was the breadwinner is also reflected in the attitude to unemployment. The state consistently refused to recognise the fact that women engaged in waged work and hence unemployment was not acknowledged as a problem affecting them. It was left to the women's movement of the late nineteenth century to focus on the hardships suffered by the unemployed female labour force. When concern over female unemployment was voiced, relief programmes were hampered by values and assumptions about what was acceptable work for women and what was the proper role of married working-class women.

The reality for working-class girls and women at the turn of the nineteenth century did not conform to the ideal of Victorian womanhood. Neither the family backgrounds nor the conditions under which they lived and worked made it possible for them to attain the appearance of being ladies. In the period 1890 to 1914 there was a major influx of women into the labour force, definitions of what constituted respectable work for women were broadened and there was increasing recognition of the importance of work in many women's lives. However, the basic ideas of a woman's place and nature remained the same. Married women were only to work as a last resort, and it was assumed that girls would marry and give up work. Entry into the labour force was considered a threat to a woman's preparation for marriage and her search for a husband. It was also considered to be an attack on the authority structure and personal relationships of the family.

Certainly, in 1850 a majority of working-class women found it necessary to engage in waged work at some time in their lives. In 1851, one in four women with husbands alive were registered as employed. This statistic errs on the low side as it excludes many casual workers and many women engaged on waged work in the home. A whole class of women were, therefore, excluded from the ideal of true womanhood and family life. However, the very class that promulgated the ideology of feminine domesticity could only aspire to its ideals through the exploitation of working-class women as factory workers, as agricultural workers, as homeworkers, as domestic servants and as prostitutes.

In the mid-nineteenth century, domestic service was in general the only employment open to single women which might give any sort of guarantee of regular employment. In 1861, one in every three women aged between fifteen and twenty-four was a domestic servant. It was an appointment which often brought with it loneliness, isolation, overwork and very little free time. An example from Lancashire illustrates that when working-class girls were presented with a viable alternative, that is between regular employment at the mills and domestic service, the former was preferred. The position of young women in the textile areas was different from other parts of the country for 'in a manufacturing town who did not prefer the better wages and greater independence of working in a Mill?'[5] Domestic service was considered more respectable than factory or agricultural work because the work was inside a home in the context of a family-type situation, and domestic servants were seen as the most protected of all working-class girls. In reality however, they were easy prey for upper- and middle-class men, and were subject to dismissal without a reference by irresponsible and uncaring mistresses.

In 1850, working-class women were employed in a large variety of tasks in agriculture in all counties but the type of work varied according to the particular traditions and customs of a locality. Women performed all kinds of tasks and worked at harvesting corn, hay, potatoes, peas, hops, turnips, beans and apples.[6] Work in the fields was extremely arduous involving long hours, often unpleasant working conditions exacerbated by unsuitable dress which convention forbade women to discard for more suitable clothing. Women's and children's earnings were very important and in many instances the family of an agricultural labourer would not have been able to subsist without them, but by the end of the nineteenth century evidence points to a decline in the employment of women in agriculture. From 1890 onwards the regularity of work for men was increasing slowly and slight improvements in wages were also occurring. The extent and type of agricultural work women were prepared to undertake seems to have changed from this time onwards. Changes in attitude coupled with greater mobility and the more extensive use of machinery on farms meant that by the turn of the century agriculture was no longer an important field of employment for women.

Work available to women in industry was perhaps more regular than that in agriculture or home industries, but seasonality was still a problem in the majority of trades. Obviously the amount of regular work varied from one industry to another, while within the factory rigid status differences existed and certain women were more likely to get regular work than others.

The industrial position of working-class women varied between areas, but the supply of female labour was always affected by the kind of work available to their menfolk. In Middlesbrough, for example, working-class women occupied a different position from women in many other manufacturing towns because practically the only large industry in the town (iron) offered no employment to women. No organised women's labour existed there.[7] The men's work was regular and wages relatively high and the women tended to marry very young. A similar situation prevailed in the mining areas. In these areas women would have had to earn a wage as charwomen or similar work, or a widow may sometimes have opened a small shop in one of the rooms of her house.

The work available to women in the textile areas differed from other female jobs in that it provided regular employment and relatively high wages. In the 1830s and 1840s the majority of these female textile workers were daughters of hand loom weavers whilst many of the married women workers were the wives of weavers, so women followed their traditional employment out of the cottage and into the factory.[8] Mechanisation transformed the traditional work and conditions of employment of women in clothing production. However, the transition was often more gradual than one might at first suppose, as is illustrated by Nancy Osterud's study of women's work in the nineteenth century hosiery industry in Leicester.[9]

The Industrial Revolution did not change the division of labour based upon gender, indeed it reinforced it. The movement of women's work into the factories created new categories of work, which were remunerated by a 'women's wage'. The relatively high wages paid to women in the northern industrial areas were an exception: the majority of female factory work was poorly paid and job security was the norm.

In 1850 women were not employed in the professions, clerical work, craft industries or business. Women's involvement in the business sphere was ended by the Industrial Revolution, which separated home from business. They were no longer employed in significant numbers in the heavy industries either: the Factory Acts, in offering protection to females and children, played their part in reinforcing a sexual division of labour in the economy. And women were seldom found in industries requiring skill and apprenticeships. A few trades such as dressmaking and millinery could mean respectability and training but apprenticeships in the more respectable branches of the trades were expensive and girls were easy prey for exploitation.

Large numbers of married women still worked in the home, often on work given out from the factories in expanding consumer trades such as clothing and boots and shoes. The traditional rural home industries continued to employ not only married women but also large numbers of single women and girls, for example in pillow-lace-making, straw-plaiting and glovemaking. Women were also working in small workshop production as assistants to their husbands, for example in shoemaking or tailoring. The multitude of home industries formed the main source of employment for the married woman, the deserted wife and the widow. The main employment for single women – residential domestic service – ended with marriage, which left the majority of married women eligible only for employment in the unskilled home industries or in the wide variety of extended domestic occupations such as cleaning, washing, mangling and taking in lodgers.

In the early twentieth century, the prevailing attitude to married women working depended on the type of work they did. Domestic work was still considered suitable, as was any form of sewing, especially if it was done in the home. Taking in washing or lodgers continued to be acceptable possibilities for married women, but factory work for married women was criticised, especially if they had children. The view that married women should not work outside the home is reflected in the oral evidence.[10]

From interviews carried out between 1975 and 1982 with women in Colchester it emerged that most of these women stopped going out to work ofter they were married although some returned when their children were older. They were asked whether they or their mothers had returned to work after they were married. Most said that married women did not work in those days, even if they then went on to say that their mother had, in fact, taken in homework.

But I never went to work after I married . . . well that was an unheard of thing in those days, wives going to work . . . you was looked down upon if you had to go to work, you were looked down upon as if you was poor.

Were they all young girls working there? (in the workshop) They'd all started from school and they worked up . . . some of them you see, they remained old maids. Only us younger ones what got married then left.

Did any of them stay on after they were married?
No, all left.
Did your mother work after she was married?

No, I don't know, they seemed to think if a woman worked after marriage . . . it was something to be ashamed of. You were looked down on. You could do it at home and they didn't take too much notice of it . . . like my mother, although she did it at home she never went *out* to work.

Did you go out to work after you were married?
No. I never went out to work after I was married. There wasn't many who did. They used to cry shame on them in them days when they were married if they went out to work. They used to say your husband should keep you. 'Course today it's different. . .

It was accepted by all the women interviewed that women could take in work at home, although this often meant working longer hours for less pay.

For women, work played a contingent role in their lives, whereas for men it was a determining force. Unmarried working-class women expected to marry. That is not to say that they produced abstract formulations of the role of marriage in their lives – they probably never considered the question in general terms at all – but it was accepted as common sense that they would marry and leave paid work. Practical considerations were also important. Marriage often meant escape from a job that was both tedious and tiring. On the other hand, they were often situated in these particular low-paid and dead-end jobs precisely because of the expectation that they *would* marry.

However, the period that women spent in the work-force was an important factor in developing their consciousness of themselves as a social group. Collective identification was problematic for women in a way it was not for men, and this had important implications for their participation in organised structures such as trade unions. Work in a factory, almost always in sex-segregated groups, was their first experience in a situation where the social position they shared as women could emerge. However, this process of collective identification, although crucial in creating conditions in which it was *possible* for women to identify with each other, did not in practice always have this effect. This was largely because of their view of work as temporary and peripheral to their lives. One cannot treat women who worked simply as members of the industrial labour force who happened to be female: the ways must be examined in which their experience has been shaped by the primacy of their family roles.[11]

As women's economic status has always been inseparably intertwined with her position in the social institution of the family, it is impossible, and indeed unrealistic, to attempt to study homeworkers purely in terms of their economic role when their waged work is inextricably linked to unpaid domestic work. In studying homewrok we are investigating a subject that helps to highlight the oppression of women in a society which has institutionalised the concept of dependency. The homeworking labour force, of whom the majority have always been unskilled female workers, has consistently formed one of the most underpaid and sweated sectors of the capitalist economy. Its recruitment has thrived on the fact that the society of post-Industrial Revolution Britain has emphasised women's dependence on male breadwinners and defined women purely in terms of their roles as wives and mothers. The concept of dependency also meant that 'respectability' came to be associated with women performing a purely domestic role which did not take them out of their 'natural' sphere. The opportunities for women to engage in waged work were, therefore, limited both by the actual narrowness in choice of employment open to them and also by pervasive social constraints. Homework helped to solve the dilemma facing many women: that is, that they needed to earn a wage but also either wished to keep this fact a secret or at least wanted to earn money within the confines of their domestic environment. Homework is also the form of waged work that combines most easily with the demands made upon a woman in her role as non-waged domestic labourer. These reasons have meant that homeworkers have been recruited not only from the working classes but also from the wives and daughters of the lower middle classes. This book will attempt to examine the homeworker as a female worker and takes as its starting point the contention that homework has not only exploited but has also, to some extent, played a part in perpetuating women's subordinate socio-economic position.[12]

2

Homeworkers: work and family life

A strategy that married women could adopt to earn money and still fulfil their family commitments was to take in homework. The varying attitudes towards women's work and specifically towards women's work in the home were important considerations in determining and influencing women's employment choices. Since the types of employment engaged in by women in the nineteenth and early twentieth centuries were determined by social as well as economic considerations, it is useful to look at both middle-class and working-class attitudes towards homework before looking in detail at the groups of women which actually made up the homework labour force.

The virtues of homework as seen through middle-class eyes are set out most clearly by Mrs Henry Wood in her novel *Mrs. Haliburton's Troubles*, which is set in a glove manufacturing district:

> Helstonleigh abounded with glove manufactories. It is a trade that may be said to be a blessing to the localities where it is carried on, since it is one of the very few employments that furnish to the poor female population easy, clean and profitable work at their own homes. The evils of women going out to work in the factories have been rehearsed over and over again; and the chief evil – we will put all others out of sight – is, that it takes the married woman from her home and family . . . But with glove making the case is different. While the husbands are abroad at the manufactories pursuing their daily work, the wives and elder daughters are earning money easily and pleasantly at home.[1]

15

It is interesting, however, to contrast this with another quotation from the same novel:

> They be the improvidentest things in the world, mum, these gloveress girls. Sunday they be decked up as good as queens, flowers inside their bonnets, and ribbons out, a-setting the churches and chapels alight with their finery; and then off for walks with their sweethearts, all the afternoon and evening.[2]

The contradictions exposed in these two quotations show the hypocrisy of a moralising middle class. We discover that not all homeworkers were exempt from middle-class criticism. In the few instances where homework failed to complete the isolation and confinement of the woman in the home, middle-class dissension was quick to make itself heard. For example, the type of criticism levelled at the glovemaking girls in Mrs Henry Wood's novel had also been voiced against the straw-plaiters. In fact, we even find one instance where homeworkers (bonnet sewers and straw-plaiters) are being compared in an unfavourable light with factory girls. The Vicar of Dunstable in 1867 was of the opinion that the morals of the Dunstable girls (a factory area) were 'Preferable to those of the girls either in Luton where they work principally in their own home or lodgings, or in the neighbouring villages where in summer they walk the lanes to plait.[3]

It is noticeable that criticism of homeworkers is directed against the single girl and not the married woman. The reasons for this are spelt out in the following remarks on the plait-girls, taken from the 1867 Royal Commission on Agriculture:

> The great want of chastity amongst the plait girls probably arises from the early age at which, when plait is good, the girls become independent of their parents and often leave their homes, and from the fact that male and female plaiters go about the lanes together in summer engaged in work which has not even the wholesome corrective of more or less physical exhaustion.[4]

When we find criticism of homeworkers, its roots stem from a dislike of any form of independence that single girls were able to attain through their work. Mrs Henry Wood and those like her were voicing criticism of the way in which these young girls were spending their leisure time and earnings. It would seem that whenever girls could earn a living wage along with leisure time to spend it, their morals came in for criticism. While women worked in the home for barely subsistence wages with no leisure time at their disposal, with overriding family responsibilities and commitments, they could be viewed as virtuous, even worthy objects of Victorian philanthropy. When girls could earn slightly more than bare subsistence wages, whether in factory, field or home, their 'betters' began to express great concern about their moral welfare. There was the ever-present fear that remunerative work would make women feel independent of, or at least equal to, their menfolk. Reasonable wages encouraged independence while also enabling girls to assert their individuality by purchasing certain article of 'finery'. Even access by working-class women to the most limited amount of control over their own lives was resented. Independence and individuality were most definitely not seen as suitable virtues to be encouraged in Victorian womanhood.

The attitude of the working class itself and the socialist and labour organisations towards women engaging in waged work in Victorian times was fairly complex. Not all the hostility directed against women engaging in industrial production necessarily stemmed from a fear of their attaining the same economic independence as men. By the middle of the nineteenth century many of the horrors that women and children had faced in the mines, mills and factories had been exposed. It was not surprising, therefore, that various individuals argued against women's work outside the home from philanthropic motives. Amongst contemporary socialists and feminists there were divergent opinions on the subject. Many socialists believed that the position of women could only be improved through the advancement of the position of men. On the other hand, some socialist feminists saw women's entry into industrial production as a pre-condition of women's emancipation. The argument of these socialist feminists was that women had to move into the productive sphere and experience the wage slavery of capitalism. Women needed to advance from their position as domestic slaves and their subordinate position of economic dependency on men.

The choice of homework can be seen as an attempt to compromise between traditional family patterns and the new economic conditions, norms and values which were being forced upon the working class by the general process and progress of the Industrial Revolution. Homework meant that greater prestige could still be attached to the male breadwinner, for as the work did not take the woman out of the home it did not conflict with her traditional sphere of activity. Women working as homeworkers were also less likely to be seen to constitute a threat to male workers as the majority of homework was viewed as 'women's work'.

———————

Which groups of women provided the sweated labour force for the homework trades and why? The type of women working as homeworkers were set out by the 1908 Select Committee on homework into three categories:

(a)   Single women, widows, wives deserted or separated from their husbands, and wives whose husbands are ill or unable to work. These are usually regular workers. They vary much in age, skill and efficiency, in the class of work they do, and the amount they are able to earn.

(b)   Wives who obtain work when their husbands are out of employment. They are more or less casual workers; some of them have not had any real training, and are unskilled. They have to take such work as is available at the moment, and such terms as are offered to them.

(c)   Wives and daughters of men in regular employment, who wish to increase the family income. They usually select pleasant work and do not ordinarily work very long hours.[5]

An analysis of the homework labour force reveals that lower-middle-class women were a significant category, but it is particularly difficult to find out anything about this group of homeworkers. Society refused to recognise their existence in the labour market and therefore their employment was not recorded: and the women themselves and their husbands were often very keen to keep the work a secret in the interests of respectability. The implications of this were that, unlike working-class homeworkers, they were not likely to come into contact with social investigators, trade unions or public and private charity organisations and hence the usual sparse channels for recording this type of work were not available vis-à-vis the middle class homeworker.

What evidence is available suggests that it was not uncommon for women with husbands in occupational categories usually associated with the lower middle class – clerks, shopkeepers and clergy, for example, – as well as the artisans (commonly seen as the most respectable and socially-aspiring section of the upper working class) to take in homework. Homework was more socially acceptable than going out to work – this meant that homeworkers came from a wider social background than we might at first suppose. Not only married women but also single girls and spinsters from the lower middle class would often take in homework as a way of maintaining themselves in as decent a manner as possible. Homework was a useful occupation for daughters of lower-middle-class men who could not easily support unmarried daughters but who naturally did not want this fact to be generally known. Homework could be a useful stop-gap for those girls until a suitable marriage partner was found. As the work could be kept a secret, or at the very worst was 'only a bit of sewing', and therefore quite respectable, it would not have impaired their marriage chances.

Widowhood was one of the major causes of poverty in Victorian and Edwardian society. The wife of a clerk or clergyman might be the very essence of respectability but the death of the husband could transform her position overnight. Although these families could be fairly comfortable while the husband was alive, his wages were seldom high enough to allow savings. So the death of the husband in a lower-middle-class family could force that family into a state of poverty. The only difference between them and the working class was their respectability, which had to be preserved at all costs. A widow from this stratum of society was unlikely to have been trained in anything except needlework and so this was the employment to which she would be forced to turn in order to support herself and perhaps children as well. Homework was often the only employment for the 'respectable widow'. A woman in such a position had to hope that she lived within call of a clean and light home industry.

It was for these reasons that lower-middle-class women and girls, not wishing to demean themselves by being seen to be competing with working-class women for employment, opted to take in

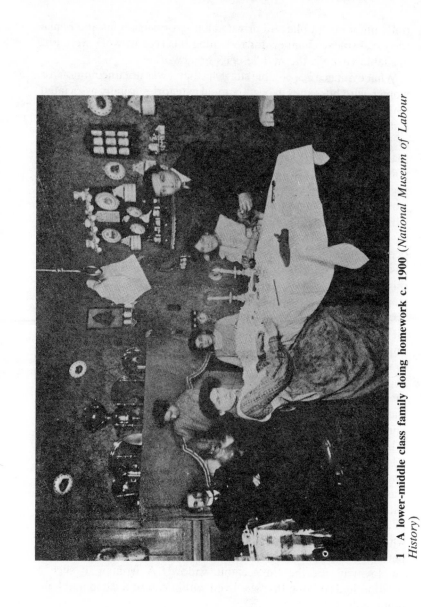

1 A lower-middle class family doing homework c. 1900 (*National Museum of Labour History*)

homework. In the middle of the nineteenth century there were few respectable alternative forms of employment for this group of women. For example, clerical and commercial work which went some way to meeting the employment demands of this sector of the female population did not become widely available until the early twentieth century. Homework's greatest advantage to the lower-middle-class women who economically needed to work and socially needed to be seen not to be working, was the fact that it could be carried on clandestinely. A servant could be sent to collect and return the work. A survey of homeworkers in London in the 1880s reported that at least half a dozen employers stated that ladies sent their servants to fetch their work and carry it back.[6]

The type of homework taken in by this group was either sewing or embroidery. It could be carried out in the privacy of the home, but in any case no one would be surprised to see a 'lady' doing some needlework during her leisure hours. Clara Collett, writing of London in the 1880s, stated that the young wife of the clerk who had regular employment but a small salary took sealskin capes home to earn extra for savings. According to Collett, these women worked for money to purchase household extras but not for a livelihood.[7] However, homework provided the extra money needed to keep up appearances. It was Collett's opinion that the women of the skilled artisan and shopkeeping strata were not ashamed of working for money but were most anxious to make it clear that they were working only for pocket money: 'pursuing a trade of their own free choice, not because they are obliged'.[8]

The 1907 study of homework in West Ham confirmed the existence of lower-middle-class homeworkers. They found that of 294 cases in which the homeworker gave her husband's occupation, 14 were clerks and 7 were tradesmen. Although they found that wives of artisans were sometimes supporting out-of-work husbands, there were still wives married to men with fairly regular and well-paid employment who took in homework to buy 'extras'.[9]

In effect, it concluded that homework itself was not accorded a high status but it enabled a number of families to maintain a higher social status and a more respectable façade than would otherwise have been possible. In this sense, homework played a part in helping to bolster up the Victorian ideal of the family and women's natural domesticity.

Perhaps this evidence also helps to support the contention that the majority of middle class women could not afford the luxury of idleness. Perhaps, however, it also confuses the issue in that we find women employing a servant but still finding it necessary to engage in waged work themselves. What it certainly does show is the pressure of needing to be seen to be conforming to an ideal that spelt respectability.

The working-class attitude towards women working was, as we have seen, by no means a homogeneous one. In many instances, the question of choice and preference did not enter into it. Married women were constantly being forced out to work, to compensate for the low or intermittent earnings or unemployment of the male breadwinner. The supply of female labour was, therefore, always to some extent affected by the kind of work available to men.[10] The wives of casual labourers (who formed a significant section of the working population in 1850) often only wanted to enter the labour market for a limited period of time. Both Charles Booth's London survey and the findings of the Select Committee on Homework in 1908 found evidence to support the contention that the supply as well as the demand for female labour fluctuated. The irregularity and seasonality which has always characterised the majority of homework trades must thus be seen in relation to fluctuations in the female labour supply. The following extract from the 1908 Select Committee report illustrates the point:

(Chairman)   So far as you are able to ascertain, what was the main reason why these people were working under these conditions which you found largely unsatisfactory? Was it owing to their personal poverty or was it owing to the uncertainty of the earnings of the head of the family where there was a man? Take a family where there was a husband and wife, was it owing to the casual employment of the head of the family?

(Mr. Howarth)   There was a great deal of evidence to show that the earnings were supplementary to the casual earnings of the head of the family, and that it is quite natural in a place like West Ham, where the casual labour is so extensive, due to the docks and low-skilled factories and so on.

(Chairman)	You would suggest that there is a larger proportion of unskilled labour in West Ham than in many parts of London?
(Mr. Howarth)	Certainly
(Chairman)	And that you think is one reason why there is so much homework to supplement the earnings of casual labour?
(Mr. Howarth)	Yes. In the cases that we visited fifty three per cent of the whole were supplementing the earnings of either casual or irregular workers.
(Chairman)	Did these people work regularly or did they work casually at all? Did they work when their husbands were in employment or did they only take up this work when their husbands were out of employment?
(Mr. Howarth)	A great many took it up definitely when their husbands were out of employment or working short hours, others took it up in order to insure against a bad time when their husbands could be out of employment, so that they would have something to fall back upon.[11]

Over half of the clothes-making homeworkers investigated in the West Ham study of 1907 were the wives of builders, general labourers and dock labourers, all of whom were prone to irregularity of employment. The following table taken from the study suggests a positive correlation between the irregular employment of the husband, and the wife taking in homework:

The usual occupations of husbands were given in 294 cases[12]

14 clerks	99 general labourers
7 tradesmen	11 carmen
42 artisans	17 mariners
13 corporation employees	16 miscellaneous
16 building trades	16 unable to work

Even where the work of the husband was fairly regular, wages were often so low as to necessitate the wife and children engaging in some form of remunerative employment. For example, agricultural labourers were notoriously badly paid and their wives and daughters were the basis of the rural home industries' labour force. Most of the women interviewed in the Colchester area were the daughters of agricultural labourers, sailors and fishermen or (in the town) builders and general labourers. It is clear from what they say that their mothers needed to take in homework in order for the family to survive:

Mrs Richards of Rowhedge (a coastal village) remembers:
'Well she (her grandmother) died in 1924 and she was 81 then and I have often thought to myself that times were jolly bad in those days because there was no money about for one thing and when the men did go to sea, when they were young and fit and when they were yachtsmen there was never very much in the winter you see . . . So that really and truly taking the biggest part of the families they were brought up, or helped to be brought up I should say by their mothers doing the tailoring at home . . . That was the only thing that the women *could* do you see. There was no transport to get into Colchester, no buses I mean, they'd got kids at home and they'd got a machine . . .'

Mrs Marsh and Mrs Petty came from Colchester:
'Yes my mother did tailoring. 'Cos she had to keep us going. Dad didn't earn very much. He was a painter and decorator and you always had to wait your money if you did anything like that because he used to work . . . up Lexden way and they don't pay like we do you see, they didn't in those days and Mum used to do coats at home from the factory. She used to work very hard for the little she got to make ends meet you see'.
'My mother did that bit of tailoring to feed us kids. She didn't do that for a bit of pocket money, she did that to keep us. She had 11 in 12 years, she had, she was having babies every year . . . My husband didn't earn a lot when we got married. I used to have £2 a week housekeeping but with my thirty bob what I could earn it helped, didn't it? That helped me buy little extras for my children that I wouldn't've been able to have given if I hadn't work, see? Yes, 'course there was no allowance for children, if you had children well that was up to you to keep 'em, which I done'.

The last extract illustrates the changes in two generations. Mrs Petty saw her mother as taking in homework from absolute necessity whilst she did homework to buy 'little extras' for the children. This reflects the rise in male wages in the early twentieth century.

The relationship of the supply of married women's labour to the state of their husbands' trades inevitably reinforced theories of women as an essentially transient sector of the labour force. In general, married women were found in the lowest-status jobs. The attractions of homework to the married working-class woman are obvious. The waged work could be carried out while she kept an eye on her children and attended to all the other demands made upon her as a wife and mother. Homework was the system that lent itself most easily to this fluctuating supply of married women's labour. In fact, homework is a system that thrives on the fact that it can expand and contract its labour force at will. It is the reservoir of married women's labour that has supplied the necessary conditions for a system of homework-based industries during the nineteenth and twentieth centuries.

The employment pattern of married women had a detrimental effect on the woman who was the sole breadwinner. The position of women attempting to maintain themselves and possibly their families all the year round on the pittance earned at homework, was indeed an especially unenviable one. Speaking of his East London parish, the Reverend Brooke Lambert stated:

I have spoken of the men who lounge round the dockyard gate, they are at least men, but what shall we say of the women, who have the same heavy burden to bear. Now, when I tell you that needlework done by the large class of East End sempstresses is paid for at an average only of three-farthings per hour, clear wage, so that working twelve to eighteen hours, it is difficult to make one shilling a day, you will see that their case is a very sad one. But if they had always this ill-paid work to do, these poor creatures would be thankful, but such are the fluctuations of trade, that they find it difficult to earn this wretched sum.[13]

It was the widow, the deserted wife of the wife with a sick or disabled husband who worked most regularly at homework and who were the greatest sufferers from seasonality and irregularity in the supply of work which characterised the majority of homework trades. Mrs Spratt's mother tried to do tailoring but her eyesight was

too bad. Left a widow with three children, she did washing and
cleaning to make ends meet:

> She used to have 24 sheets at a time, different people – 1½d each
> it was in them days. She did work hard. She was only 39 when she
> was left with us three. No help in them days. She used to go to
> work from 9 till 12 for 9d. – go out charring. She used to get up at 5
> o'clock in the morning and do some work – washing. Leave off
> and get to work by 9 come at one . . . That was hard work in them
> days and bad pay.

Single working-class women made up a substantial section of the
homework labour force, but especially in the rural districts where
little or no alternative employment was available. A home industry
such as straw plaiting, glovemaking or lace-making would
commonly be preferable to residential domestic service which often
meant leaving one's family, friends and community.

The children of working-class parents were also a very important
category of home labour in both rural and urban home industries.
They could be found in large numbers in country districts working at
straw-plaiting, pillow-lace-making and glovemaking, or in the town
helping parents or neighbours make up matchboxes, or card hooks
and eyes, buttons and pins. Although the pay for homework was
always very low the combined work of a wife and children could
result in a remuneration equivalent to that of the husband in a
poorly paid occupation such as that of agricultural labourer.

Mrs Potter came from a large family in Colchester and the
children all helped their mother with the tailoring:

> *Before the war did your mother ever take in tailoring at home?*
> Yes! I was born with a needle and cotton in my hand. She used to
> do the finishing. My Aunt Miriam used to machine the trousers
> and we kids used to have to go down there and get these and bring
> 'em back and my mother would put the pockets in and the buttons
> on. My mother used to say; 'Well, its your turn to stop up
> tonight'. That's me. And she said: 'You can sort the buttons out
> for me.' I used to sort the buttons out what she was putting on the
> trousers and then she'd say, 'If you get a needle and cotton, you
> can put some on.' Ooh, I'd say, that'd be nice. I thought that was
> lovely. I thought I was doing her a good turn, well I was really.

The children used to fetch and carry the tailoring for their mothers especially in rural areas:

> Mr Jones, the carrier's cart used to bring it out and sometimes we had to walk to town with a bundle of coats done if mother wanted the money. We used to go and take the coats and walk to Colchester with them . . . Yes it was an awful long way, wasn't it?
> *Did you children use to help her in other ways?*
> We used to press the seams and the sleeves . . . when we came home from school.

Mrs Gow remembered that her mother used to have to walk to Colchester and back with the tailoring on the pram:

> Of course, before I was big enough to take it on they used to have to take it and walk into Colchester with it on the prams. I remember all of that and from Eight Ash Green to Lexden there wasn't a house nowhere. It was all plain and dark and my mother and Mrs Bailey . . . they trudged along with the prams to take this in . . . And then they'd bring it back, once a week.
> Them days were terrible. After, when I did it they brought the van out. I should never have done that.
> *They must've been desperate.*
> They were hard times then, you know.

During the second half of the nineteenth century there was a large supply of women who for a variety of reasons could not, or did not wish to, work outside the home. Many of these were married women whose mobility was greatly restricted by their husbands' economic and social status and their domestic responsibilities. The majority of women were not trained for any particular trade, but they could usually turn their hand to homework, which was generally seen as unskilled work. Women returning to the labour market after a long period in the isolation of the home also turned to homework, being unable to compete with young girls or single women in the few alternative fields of employment open to them. For example, a large number of elderly women who would have been rejected if they had applied for any other form of employment were eager to take in homework:

Said an old woman, a maker of crêpe flowers, to me one day, 'If I was to go askin' for work at the warehouse they wouldn' give it to me, they'd say – you're no good, you're too old! But I know how to do these 'ere flowers better nor the young 'uns.[14]

An analysis of the categories of women taking in homework and their reasons for choosing homework clearly illustrates that women's social status in society spills over into the economic sphere and in this instance results in the formation of a captive labour force upon which a system of homeworking is entirely dependent. Conversely, women's weak economic status, achieved by denying her access to the better-paid and more skilled jobs and the association of 'women's work' with unpaid homework, brand women as subordinate creatures inferior to and dependent on men.

2 **Artificial-flower-making at home.** *Daily News Sweated Industries Exhibition Catalogue (1906) (National Museum of Labour History)*

3

Homework and economic change, 1850–1914

The purpose of this chapter is to try to define homework and situate it in a particular stage of the historical development of industrialisation.

From the sixteenth to the eighteenth centuries the domestic system of manufacture predominated in England and the clothing and textile industries were almost totally reliant on outworkers, weaving and spinning being the major outwork proccesses. In general, weaving was the work of men who worked in their own homes. Spinning, on the other hand, was predominantly the work of women and was a true 'cottage industry'. The spinners were most often sweated labourers working on materials given out by the employer. It was monotonous and repetitive work labelled as unskilled women's work and carrying a very low status. The spinners were unorganised and completely at the mercy of their employers.

Under the domestic system of manufacture. employers usually gave out the raw materials but the workers owned their own machines. The system differed from the preceding guild system where the workers were independent producers owning their own raw materials and their own machines. The whole relationship between employer and employee was transformed under the domestic system. The worker also had to sell his or her labour power. The medieval guilds had prohibited journeymen from taking work home and from working for more than one master. This was to protect their status and bargaining position and to guard against journeymen becoming 'mere outworkers'. With the collapse of the guild system, outwork became the generalised form of production. A transition from one system of production to another is obviously gradual and subject to an unevenness in development, so different systems of production often co-exist. The Industrial Revolution tht occasioned the transition from the domestic unit of manufacture to the capitalist system of production can only be said to have made the factory the *predominant form* of industrial organisation.

The term outwork is most often assocciated with the domestic system of manufacturing. It is a system which predominated when the family was the major unit of production. Although women were excluded from entry into the crafts they worked in a variety of traditional home or cottage industries such as lacemaking, straw-plaiting or button-making. Outwork as we understand it under the domestic system of manufacture had little in common with what Karl Marx has termed the modern domestic industry of capitalism.

'Modern domestic industry', 'in which capital conducts it exploitation in the background of modern mechanical industry', cannot be understood as a mere transitional form between the domestic system of manufacture and the factory system of production. Domestic industry under capitalism is not a mere legacy or anachronism dating from an earlier form of production. 'Modern domestic industry' provides an example of one of the intermediate forms which 'are here and there reproduced in the background of Modern Industry, though their physiognomy is totally changed'.[2]

The worker in 'modern domestic industry' generally owns neither the machinery nor the raw materials. In order to subsist he or she must sell his or her labour power:

> Capitalist outwork may be said to be fully established only when the material belongs to the trading employer, and is returned to him after the process for which the outworker's skill is required has been completed – the wool to be given out to be spun, the yarn to be given out to be woven, the shirt given out for 'seam and gusset and band', the nail-rod to be returned as nails, the limbs to be returned as dolls, the leather coming back as boots.[3]

The transistion from the domestic to the factory system witnessed a radical change in the composition and life-style of the labour force:

In contrast with the manufacturing period, the division of labour is thenceforth based, wherever possible, on the employment of women, of children of all ages, and of unskilled labourers, in one word, on cheap labour, as it is characteristically called in England. This is the case not only with all production on a large scale, whether employing machinery or not, but also with the so-called domestic industry, whether carried on in the houses of the workpeople or in small workshops. The old-fashioned domestic industry has now been converted into an outside department of the factory, the manufactory, of the warehouse. Besides the factory operatives, the manufacturing workmen and the handicraftsman whom it concentrates in large masses at one spot, and directly commands, capital also sets in motion, by means of invisible threads another army; that of the workers in the domestic industries, who dwell in the large towns and are also scattered over the face of the country.[4]

The modern domestic industry or system of homeworking is dependent on the exploitation of a cheap and immature labour-power, that is, predominantly women and children. A skilled artisan no longer makes a product throughout but the job is broken down into a number of detail processes often demanding only unskilled labour. Each worker carries out a specific operation and together these workers make up the productive labour force of the capitalist system of producton, of which homeworkers are an integral part.

Modern domestic industry is not separate from and independent of the factory system. The dominant tendency towards centralisation developed unevenly, as illustrated by the scope of modern domestic industry in the nineteenth century. The Industrial Revolution is the process commonly associated with steam power and mechanisation, bringing with it increased productivity of labour and cheaper commodities. However, we cannot entirely equate the period of the Industrial Revolution with a purely factory-based system and the disappearance of workshops, home industries and hand-work.[5] Indeed, for much of the nineteenth century there was a form of combined development of hand and machine production. It was a time in which, despite the movement towards concentration of production in factories and the growth of large firms, there was also an increase in production based on smaller economic units. The

Industrial Revolution was a force that led not only to centralisation of production but also in certain areas of the economy, to a greater fragmentation of production. As D. S. Landes argues in his study of technological change and industrial development in Western Europe,the very forces that promoted industrial and commercial giantism opened up a new possibilities for small ventures; service enterprises, distribution agencies, sub-contractors and so on.[6]

In the eighteenth and nineteenth centuries mechanisation was an uneven and sporadic process taking place in different industries at varying rates. Capitalist enterprise took quite different forms, depending on the specific character of the industry itself. The nineteenth century clothing industry is the most obvious example of an industry on which the Industrial Revolution acted as a centrifugal rather than centripetal force.

Whereas in the textile industries expansion and growth took the form of concentration of plant and workers into vast factories, the clothing industry combined large factories with a plethora of small workshops and masters, and a multitude of homeworkers. What, then, were the reasons for the slow advancement of mechanisation? Why did homework not only survive under the new economic conditions but actually increased in a number of industries and trades during the nineteenth century? Finally, what factors were responsible for the demise of many of the home industries during the latter part of the nineteenth century?

Let us look first of all at the question of mechanisation and its relevance to homework. The nineteenth century was a period of industrial expansion that inevitably altered organisation and techniques of production and provided the conditions in which a wide variety of forms of economic organisation could co-exist with a great variety of conditions of work. It was a time in which it was discovered that industrial expansion could be achieved through combining factory work with homework and that direct competition between machine and hand production need not always prevail: certain technical innovations actually increased the volume of homework, in fact a prime example of this is the sewing machine. The sewing machine was a response to radical technological changes in production in other spheres of the clothing and textile industries. A transition to machine-produced spinning made mechanised weaving a necessity, and the mechanisation in the production of the raw materials of clothing necessitated the introduction of machinery in the making-up of clothes in order to keep pace. However, the invention of the sewing machine did not mean a transition to a wholly factory-based clothing industry. On the contrary, it provides an example showing how the introduction of certain technology facilitated the growth of homework. It enabled unskilled homeworkers to do work which had previously only been done by skilled workers, and thus the cost of labour power was greatly reduced.

Throughout the first half of the nineteenth century there was scarcely any device to which inventors gave more attention than the sewing machine. No satisfactory machine was designed until the late 1840s, however, and production in large numbers did not come about until nearly 1860.[7] In the case of the sewing machine it is difficult to say how much the slow development of technological change in the clothing industry was due to the failure to solve the technical problems associated with the development of the sewing machine, how far it was due to the hostility of the craftsmen-tailors to the development of machinery, and how far it was due to the fact that machinery is slow to develop in an industry where there is a readily available supply of cheap labour. However, it is interesting to note that even in the bigger tailoring factories mechanisation was only partial until well into the twentieth century. Before this the use of machinery was mainly restricted to suits and coats. It was not used in the millinery and dressmaking trades and nearly all finishing processes in every branch of the tailoring trade were done by hand until after 1910. There is no doubt that the sewing machine increased the amount of homework in ready-made clothing industry, so technical progress did not necessarily displace homeworkers, although it often altered the type of work undertaken. Many delicate and small-scale operations lent themselves to homework.[8]

In considering whether to opt for mechanisation, many factors had to be considered by the employer: the type of product and process involved was obviously an essential determining factor. Mechanisation was expensive and did not always mean a substantial gain in productivity. The intricacy of a process might have been such that machinery would not greatly speed up production. In such instances it was sometimes better to obtain a greater intensity of production through hand labour and 'sweating' of the work-force. For example, the boot and shoe industry combined centralised production for the skilled processes with decentralised production for the unskilled processes. Complete mechanisation in the boot

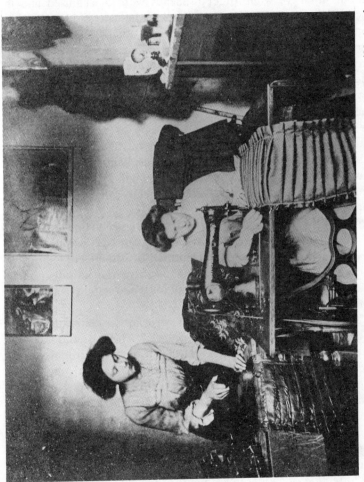

3 Skirt-making. *Daily News Sweated Industries Exhibition Catalogue* (1906) *(National Museum of Labour History)*

and shoe industry would have meant a specialised machine for each of the very different processes involved. It would have been difficult to perfect a machine for each process all at the same time and it therefore made economic sense that certain branches remained labour intensive while other branches were mechanised and in factories.[9] A specialised machine-making industry did not develop until the middle of the nineteenth century and not until then could the problems of mechanising many hand processes really be tackled. Machinery had therefore not always developed to perform the degree of intricacy required in the production of certain articles. For example, in hosiery, 'fancy' works was mechanised much later than plain work. The type of goods and consumer preference could be an important element in the decision of whether or not to mechanise. Better results could often be obtained from hand labour: superior quality goods were usually hand-made outside the factory. In tailoring, for example, a mainly hand technology lingered on at the top because human skill could not readily be replaced by machines and at the bottom because of the plentiful supply of cheap labour.[10] Thus women continued to find homework in those trades dependent upon hand labour such as pillow-lace-making, fancy hosiery work and knitting. In a number of industries, therefore, homework thrived as a result of the introduction of machinery and survived as a result of the continuation of a demand for hand-labour.

The cost and supply of labour was a crucial consideration as far as the survival of homework was concerned. There is no doubt that cheap labour can act as a deterrent to the introduction of mechanisation as can a surplus and immobile labour supply. The predominantly female labour force that was recruited for nineteenth-century home industries was all of these things. Low and irregular earnings for male workers, the surplus of women, the shortage of alternative employment open to women and girls all combined to ensure a cheap and plentiful supply of female labour. This surplus of labour encouraged manufacturers to economise in the direction of capital investment, to become labour rather than capital-intensive. Productivity could often be increased through a more systematic exploitation of labour. For example, in London where high rents, relatively high wages and high fuel costs mediated against the introduction of large-scale factory production, employers went into competition with the provinces by making use of homeworkers. This enabled them to become competitive by economising on rent, wages and machinery. London developed as a centre for a number of home industries, but in particular the ready-made clothing trades, and it provides an example of the conditions which could make homework a more viable economic proposition than factory work. The productivity of labour could be increased through the process known as 'sweating' as it was in the London clothing trades. For example, tailoring developed in marked contrast to the textile industries, where the machinery of factory industry had restructured the industries to suit a developing capitalist economy. However, in tailoring, before the development of the sewing machine, the growth of piece-work and sweated outwork had the same effect– the displacement of skilled (usually male) workers who made whole garments by cheap, unorganised (usually female) workers, making only parts of garments.[11]

One element of 'sweating' was the use of child labour. An elaborate division of labour, and hence simplification of the majority of processes in many industries, meant that labour costs could be kept to a minimum by dependence on unskilled homeworkers and child labour. This ability to make use of unpaid family labour, of child labour was important in the expansion of the clothing industries and was common in many other trades such as the hand-made and machine-made branches of the lace industry, in straw-plaiting, in the Birmingham small metal trades and in matchbox making. In processes where child labour could be used there was therefore an incentive to stay with homework and evade the restrictions of statutory legislation. The employer was also relieved of the cost of providing control and work discipline *vis-a-vis* child labour when they were employed in the home. Supervision of child labour fell to the parents, as did the cost of training, in such old country industries as for example, pillow-lace-making and straw-plaiting.

The terrible conditions ensuing from the Industrial Revolution and the introduction of a whole series of Factory Acts and protective legislation also promoted fragmentation of production and encouraged the growth of homework. The limitations on working hours and regulation of standards in the workplace was a positive incentive to employers to put work out into the one workplace unfettered by restrictive legislation. When the Factory

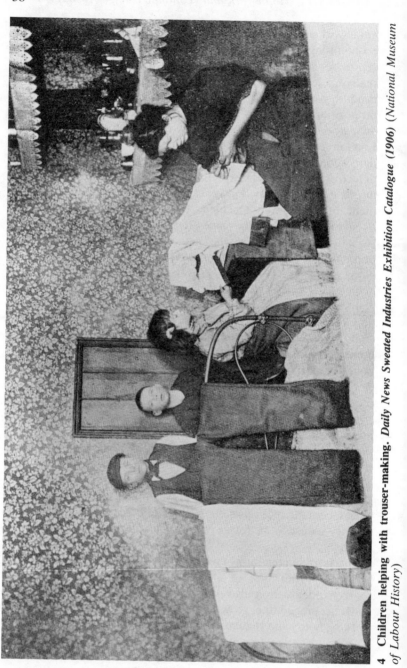

4 **Children helping with trouser-making.** *Daily News Sweated Industries Exhibition Catalogue* (1906) (*National Museum of Labour History*)

and Workshops Acts attempted to offer some protection to female and child labour, employers, in a labour-intensive industry such as the clothing industry, reluctant either to lose their cheap labour supply or to accept the restrictions placed upon its use, were encouraged to look more and more towards a homeworking labour force. The Industrial Revolution, in bringing large numbers of workers together in factories, made possible the growth of trade unionism. However, the increasing strength of the unions could also have acted as a further stimulus towards decentralisation of production. The presence of non-unionised homework labour force strengthened the position of the employer and weakened the bargaining position of the union inside the factory. Decentralisation of production in an industry could therefore inhibit the growth of trade unionism and assist the employer in keeping wages low.

The type of market conditions prevailing in the nineteenth century were an important stimulus to the survival and expansion of homework. Adverse market conditions could inhibit rapid expansion in technical innovation. A great deal of the increasing demand for consumer goods involved the clothing industries and those industries allied to it. This meant that there were great fluctuations in demand according to season and changes in fashion (for example, in tailoring, boots and shoes, hosiery and lace-making). This was a period which witnessed the extension of fashion into a new and cheaper mass-produced range of commodities. The market uncertainties, the trade cycles and seasonal demand meant that in many industries caution prevailed and products were made only in relatively small quantities at a time. Subcontraction and seasonal employment of homeworkers were important factors in dealing with erratic demands and rush orders. Labour was more flexible than machinery and particularly so if it took the form of a glut of unskilled outdoor labour. Further, the whims of fashion could be shortlived and erratic and thus it would not have been profitable or feasible to attempt to cope with those changes through adaptation of machinery. The use of home-labour meant that the employer was not forced to stock-pile goods which might soon be out of fashion. It also spared him the cost of storage.

One of the most important economic developments affecting the demand for home labour in the nineteenth century was the increase in consumer demand. The working class became important as consumers for mass-produced clothes, boots, shoes and furniture.

The nature of production shifted from producing for the individual consumer to producing for a mass market. In clothing and footwear the emphasis shifted from retail to wholesale, from bespoke to ready-made. An expansion in demand was also stimulated by greater institutional demand from organisations such as the army, navy and railway companies for uniforms, boots and other equipment. The earliest market for ready-made clothing was provided by sailors, when the work was given out to London dockers' wives in 1810.[12] A further incentive to expansions was the growth of large export markets for clothing, boots, shoes and other products.

New areas particularly suitable for adaptation to homework also developed as a direct result of changes in consumer demand; one of the most important of these was the growth in retailing and distribution. The packaging of goods is a prime example of an area that particularly lends itself to home labour. The making-up of boxes, the carding of hooks and eyes, safety pins and buttons was light, repetitive and unskilled work which developed to meet the new demand created by mass production and retailing.

What were the changing conditions that led to the decline of so many of the nineteenth-century home industries and to the disappearance of the homework sector in other trades? Changing market conditions were clearly important, as were free trade policies. A number of foreign markets failed to continue to expand and others were severely contracted during the latter part of the nineteenth century and the First World War. As the nineteenth century progressed there was also increasing foreign competition. For example, the importation of foreign plait was instrumental in the decline of the straw plait industry in this country. From around 1870 the importance of homework in industry generally seemed to be on the wane. It had previously been possible to meet a large component of the rising demand for goods through an expansion of homework, but by the latter part of the century demand for consumer goods and growth in the export trade had in a number of industries outstripped the capacity of homework to deal with it. In the field of mechanisation itself many advances had been made. Many more machines were operated by steam power, so that the problems of whether to introduce the machine into the home or factory no longer arose to the same extent. A demand for greater efficiency and rationalisation in a more competitive modern industry meant that homework with its attendant difficulties such as the risk of embezzlement of materials, the difficulty of quality control, and difficulty of ensuring that delivery dates and schedules were met, seemed more of an anachronism.

Decline in the availability of cheap labour was another 'nail in the coffin' for many home industries. A slower population growth, rising affluence, more regular work for men, the greater mobility of the rural population and a larger amount of respectable and alternative employment opening up to girls and single women were all important factors in this decline. Compulsory schooling, beginning with the 1870 Education Act, was responsible for removal of child labour as a considerable element in the pool of cheap labour. This affected many of the home industries, both urban and rural, but its withdrawal was particularly noticeable in the country industries of pillow-lace-making and straw-plaiting.

A number of other factors influenced the decline of homework at this time. The male trade union movement launched a concerted campaign against homework, which was seen as synonymous with low wages, poor working conditions and a weakening of the workers bargaining position. For example, in the boot and shoe industry, male workers had previously been reluctant to transfer work to the factories and had organised against it. By the 1890s, they had reversed their policy and were campaigning for total abolition of outwork. The boot and shoe industry provided an example of an industry in which the strength of the union meant that they were relatively successful in their campaign to abolish outwork, although employers still used homeworkers in busy times.[13]

At the same time as the male trade union movement was campaigning for the abolition of homework, women's social and labour organisations, social reformers and philanthropists were campaigning against the sweating of homeworkers and for statutory legislation to control working conditions and rates of pay. The publicity campaign and eventual legislation played an important part in the decline in the use of home labour.[14]

The saving on capital meant that homework appealed not only to the larger manufacturer but also to many small employers. Indeed, the employing of homeworkers was a valuable way up for those to espoused the ideology of the self-made man. A further saving to the employer was made on supervisory costs. The employer of homeworkers had no need to spend his own time supervising work or to employ a supervisory staff. If work was handed in below standard the homeworker was fined or required to do the work again free of charge. Supervision to ensure a guaranteed rate of production and intensity of labour is unnecessary with the piece-work system.

One of the great incentives to employ homeworkers is the tremendous flexibility of production that they allow to the entrepreneur. In the nineteenth century, when many industries were greatly affected by seasonality in demand for the products and seasonality in the supply of raw materials, this was a particularly important factor. This is, of course, still the major attraction of homework in today's clothing industry. Homework is a far more flexible system than factory production. Employers can readily halt production in times of depression and just as easily increase it in times of prosperity.

Freedom from outside intervention is an important bonus for employers. The employer of homeworkers has always had a free hand in the exploitation of his labour force. It has worked to the employer's advantage that the relationship between employer and homeworkers is commonly a clandestine one. Employers have been able to flout the Factory and Workshop Acts and any legislation designed to protect the worker through making use of a home labour force. The absence of unionisation and the socio-economic structural position of the homeworkers has always made the employer/employee relationship an especially unequal one. By putting work out to homeworkers, employers have avoided meeting recognised standards of safety, heating, lighting and sanitation as laid down by parliament. The employer of homeworkers pays only for time spent productively. As trade unions bargained for holiday pay, overtime rates, sick benefit, lunch and tea breaks, the working conditions and terms of employment of homeworkers worsened relative to those of indoor labour. For employers, however, the incentives to employ homeworkers increased with the growing influence of the trade unions on the conditions of employment of indoor labour.

There are certain disadvantages in employing homeworkers. The major disadvantage of a homework labour force is the difficulty of obtaining uniformity of production without constant supervision and using different techniques and types of machinery. Only certain light industries lend themselves to home production and the majority of home industries involve very simple processes. It is not, for example, difficult or necessarily even important to obtain uniformity of production in the carding of hooks and eyes or the making of matchboxes. The difficulty most often arises where machinery is involved and homeworkers are unable to keep up with constant advances in technology.

A further disincentive to employing homeworkers is the greater difficulty of ensuring that work is done on time and to the right standard in order to meet employers' own deadlines. Failure to meet deadlines could result in lost custom for the employer. Where this is an important consideration a factory labour force may provide a better proposition.

Only certain types of labour-intensive industries lend themselves to homework, and it is only possible in those industries where either no machinery is necessary or where the machinery can be easily adapted for use in the home. Often only the most unskilled work can profitably be put out to homeworkers: work requiring specific expertise may have to be confined to the factory. It is also more difficult to train a homework labour force. In the factory an employer can train a group of workers and introduce them to new machinery and new processes: it is not possible to be as innovatory with a homework labour force. This could be a potential disadvantage for the employer in that it could inhibit expansion and make it more difficult for him to keep pace with his competitors. Of course, not all homeworkers are unskilled. For example, embroidery, knitting and lacework can be very skilled work when done by hand. However, these workers cannot produce on the same scale of factory production and the possibility for expansion is limited.

4

Types of homework

This chapter looks at the places where homework was carried out during the period 1850–1914. It looks at those factors influencing the supply and demand for homework labour in specific areas of the country. It also looks in detail at the work processes involved in some of the most important of the nineteenth-century home industries (see the map opposite).

In the mid-nineteenth century, four major conditions determined the availability of a female labour force for recruitment to the sweated home industries. First, there were those areas of the country where men's wages were especially low; second, those districts where seasonal or casual labour was a prevalent employment pattern for men; third, those areas where no alternative employment was available to women; and fourth, areas where there was a marked surplus of women. Where one or more of these conditions prevailed employers experienced little difficulty in recruiting a home-based labour force. Employers were also attracted to those areas where a previously trained labour force was available. They were attracted to areas where there was no competition for better-paid female employment, and were drawn towards districts where a glut of female labour existed and supply was in excess of demand.

Many of the most important and long-established home industries flourished in the rural areas. This is not surprising as agricultural labourers continued to be one of the larges occupational groups and one of the lowest paid until the last quarter of the nineteenth century. Agricultural labourers in general were adversely affected by the Industrial Revolution. Their standard of

Key:
① Clothing, ② Boots and shoes, ③ Glove-making, ④ Hosiery, ⑤ Lace, ⑥ Straw-plaiting,
⑦ Box-making, ⑧ Carding, ⑨ Chain-making, ⑩ Nail-making, ⑪ Button-making

Map showing distribution of the major home industries 1850–1901

living fell during the period 1800–34 with a decline in real wages, particularly in the south and west.[1]

Wives and daughters of agricultural labourers therefore needed to make an economic contribution. This is an important factor in helping to explain the large numbers of women available to work in the three industries employing the greatest numbers of rural homeworkers. For example, in 1861 the national female straw-plaiting workforce amounted to 27 739 and in 1871, 45 270. The majority of the labour force in glovemaking, straw-plaiting and lace-making were the wives and daughters of agricultural labourers. In the second half of the nineteenth century glovemaking was found in parts of Somerset, Oxfordshire, Wiltshire, Herefordshire and Dorset. Straw-plaiting and lace-making counties overlapped. The former was to be found in Buckinghamshire, Bedfordshire, Essex, Hertfordshire, Suffolk and Cambridgeshire and the latter in Buckinghamshire, Bedfordshire, Devon, Oxfordshire and North-amptonshire. These home industries were concentrated in the areas of the country where agricultural labourers' wages were at their lowest.

Nineteenth-century London provides the most striking example of a district in which a system of casual male labour created a labour supply ideally suited to homeworking. During the second half of the nineteenth century the supply of unskilled labour in London was chronically in excess of demand.[2] A system of casual labour predominated.[3]

London was the centre for homework in the clothing industry, but many other home industries also flourished there: for example, cardboard box making, matchbox making, sack making, artificial flower making, umbrella and parasol making, fur pulling, brushmaking and tennis ball covering.

Perhaps the best example of a homework industry thriving as a result of the absence of alternative employment for women, is provided by Cradley Heath chainmaking in the Black Country. Chainmaking is heavy manual work and could in no way be seen as a typically female occupation. However, there were between two and three thousand women employed in this trade in the 1890s. The Select Committee on Sweating reported in 1888, that there was no other employment in the district for women who work at this trade and it appears to be falling more and more into their hands'.[4]

5 Mattress stuffing 1890 (*National Museum of Labour History*)

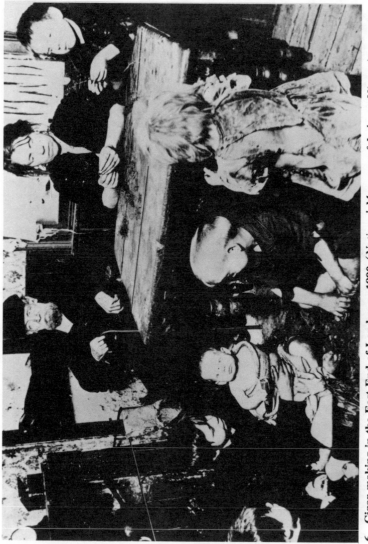

48

6 Cigar-making in the East End of London c. 1890 (*National Museum of Labour History*)

By the second half of the nineteenth century prospects for female employment in rural areas were even graver than in the towns. A certain amount of casual work in the fields, particular at harvest times, was available, but this did not provide a regular source of income. Homework was, therefore, eagerly sought by women in the country areas. Single women and country girls had little option other than to leave their homes and enter residential domestic service.

In marked contrast to rural areas such as Cradley Heath and Essex, homework was a rarity in towns such as Manchester, where well-paid and regular female employment was available in the mills. In general, those women who could not find work in the mills went out 'charring'. There was no huge reservoir of unskilled female labour to attract the homework employer. Even after marriage many women could still find work in the mills. No doubt the tradition of industrial militancy, higher wages and greater independence of women in the industrial North also created conditions in which it would have been difficult to recruit the passive, and docile labour force associated with homework.

Homework also tended to do well in those areas of the country where there was a surplus of women. For example, a great deal of homework was carried out in Nottingham where the surplus of women was particularly marked. In 1901 there were 16 000 more females than males in Nottingham. Lace and hosiery were the two major industries and employed female labour both inside and outside the factories. Certain processes required factory conditions and a predominantly female labour force was instrumental here in keeping labour costs down. At the same time, many processes – for example, those involved in 'finishing' – could easily be given out to the large numbers of women preferring to work in their own homes, thus keeping labour costs to a minimum.

A further factor for the employer to take into account was that of actual physical space and potential sites for his industry. For example, space was at a premium in London and rents were very high. An industry based predominantly on homework made the least demands on space and hence kept overhead costs to a minimum but enabled the employer to benefit from the many advantages of being London-based.

The presence of a ready-trained labour force could sometimes be a decisive factor on the demand side. While the majority of homework trades required little training or skill, there were exceptions: straw-plaiting, pillow-lace-making and glovemaking all required a certain amount of training. Specific sectors of homework industries, most often based in the towns, such as box or umbrella-making, also demanded a certain knowledge of the trade. The homework employer has never accepted the responsibility and expense of training workers.

Straw-plaiting, lace-making and glovemaking were long-established home industries by the mid-nineteenth century. Until the latter part of the nineteenth century, tradition ensured that each new generation of females was brought up with the expectation that they would work at a particular home industry. Knowledge and skill were not only passed on from mother to daughter but in certain counties special schools were established to teach the skill of the predominant home industry. In the straw-plaiting, glovemaking and pillow-lace-making counties employers not only had a ready-trained labour force but also a pool of labour that had indeed been trained for nothing else.

Homeworking and subcontracting were forms of industrial organisation favoured by the light clothing trades which came into their own during the middle decades of the late nineteenth century.[6] The bulk of the homework in clothing was machining and finishing. In whatever section of the clothing trade, whether in shirts, vests, trousers or blouses, women homeworkers were found in the worst paid jobs. For example, shirtmaking was low status work. It employed two classes of homeworker, the machinist and the finisher, and both were considered unskilled. Numbers of London's East End seamstresses made working men's shirts of harvard or flannelette (harvard is a stiff material and therefore unpleasant to sew). The West End shirt and collar trade was significantly better paid, but shirt finishers were the worst paid.

Although London formed the heart of the light clothing trade, seamstresses were found working all over England. For example, Essex was another important area for the clothing industry.[7] The low wages of the agricultural labourers in Essex forced women in the labour market and clothes were sent from Manchester, East London and Leicester to be made up in Essex. In Bristol in the 1890s, the wholesale clothing industry also employed a larger number of women than any other trade. The Royal Commission on

Labour claimed that more than three-quarters of the work for Bristol clothiers was done by a female labour force working in their own homes. An inspection of the registers of six clothing factories revealed the names of two thousand homeworkers, but the Commission estimated that doubling of the figure would produce a more accurate estimate. This revised estimate would have meant that the proportion of homeworkers to factory workers in Bristol would have been 5 : 1.[8]

The other major sector of the clothing industry to employ large numbers of homeworkers was the boot and shoe trade. The nineteenth-century boot and shoe industry was found in London, Leicester, Northampton, Bristol, Leeds, Norwich and Stafford and the second half of the nineteenth century not only witnessed the mechanisation of the light clothing trade but also of the boot and shoe industry.

Manufacturers of boots and shoes cut out the materials and gave the work to subcontractors. The homework was always very irregular and particularly so during the winter months. Three of the processes commonly done as homework were closing (sewing together the upper parts, which was easily done by machine); making (the attaching of the sole and heel to the uppers); and finishing. Finishing involved a variety of tasks such as knifing, cleaning, lining, sewing on buttons and packing.

The introduction of machinery led to an increased use of unskilled female homework labour. For example, the machine for closing introduced in the 1860s, was well-established in both the ready-made and bespoke trade by the 1880s. Like the ordinary sewing machine it was fairly small, cheap and relatively simple to operate and hence easily adaptable for work in the home. Closing was thus transformed from a skilled male preserve to a predominantly unskilled female task. The mechanisation of the finishing processes (for example, a machine for setting eyelets) also led to an increasing division of labour and, coupled with the growth in the ready-to-wear boot and shoe trade, an expansion in demand for homeworkers in finishing took place.

The women's work was nearly always seen as unskilled. One respondent, the son of a shoemaker in Hackney, and one of fourteen children, remembers the injustices suffered by women homeworkers in his own family. For example, he recalls that his aunt worked at home as a machinist of shoe uppers:

I remember I used to go round to her house quite a lot, and she used to machine the shoe uppers you see, and they used to get three and sixpence per gross, for stitching – machine – shoe – uppers together. It was absolute slavery. And they'd work till midnight and past midnight to get a living. And I can see it now quite clearly, all the shoe uppers being machined and all run off on a machine, all joined together, not time to cut them apart. When you finished one you let the thread go straight on you see until perhaps the shuttle runs out then you've got to refill your shuttle. It was absolute slavery. And three and sixpence per gross. And they reckoned, you know, that was a good pay then.[9]

It was common for whole families to do homework in the boot and shoe trade.

Although sack-sewing was not a branch of the clothing industry it deserves mention here because it was after all, needlework. When we think of the sewing trades we tend to think of clean and light work. For the homeworker this picture was often very far from the truth. A great deal of needlework was on heavy and coarse materials. Certainly sack-sewing was one of the most unpleasant of the sewing trades. It involved making new sacks or mending and reconditioning old ones. The docks provided a high demand for this trade in London. A large number of sack-sewers were therefore recruited from the East End and in particular the poorest districts such as Stepney.

The sacks had to be sewn down both sides and hemmed along the top. It was very hard work and women's hands were often cut and sore from the tar rope and coarse needles. One investigator reported that a woman had sprained both her wrists while making coal sacks for ships. Each of the coal sacks had four splices, eight holes and two patches. They had to be sewn and roped and a large 'R' worked on to them. One woman claimed that it took her two hours to complete one sack for which she received 4¾d.[10] Twenty years later Clementina Black, in her study of married women's work, discovered a fifty-year-old widow making sacks at home for 6d. and 8d. a time. In order to subsist she was forced to take in washing and also received four shillings Poor Law Relief. A married woman, with a husband in hospital, made small sacks at home for 1½d. a dozen and managed to earn seven to eight shillings a week. She received eight shillings Poor Relief and from this had to keep

7 Sack-making in the East End of London. *Daily News Sweated Industries Exhibition Catalogue (1906)* (*National Museum of Labour History*)

herself and four children.[11] The mending of old sacks was slightly better paid because the work was so much more unpleasant.

Glovemaking was an important home industry in a variety of rural areas. In the nineteenth century it was to be found in Wiltshire, Herefordshire, Oxfordshire, Worcestershire, Yeovil and Leicestershire. Worcestershire and Yeovil had the largest shares in glove production. Particular counties tended to specialise in certain types of glove and catered for different demands. Leicestershire was the centre for the woollen and worsted glove industry; Woodstock in Oxfordshire was famous for a hardwearing glove made from deerskin or sheepskin. Up to the First World War the army provided the main market for gloves to the Woodstock industry: they wore strong leather gloves of English sheepskin which were pipe-clayed to give them a very white appearance.[12] These were hand-sewn by the homeworkers, mainly the daughters and wives of agricultural labourers. Glovemaking could be light ad clean work, or it could be less pleasant work on rougher and coarser materials, as used, for example, in gardeners' and farm labourers' gloves.

As in the other clothing trades, the adaptability of the sewing machine for home use prevented glovemaking becoming entirely factory-based. In the earlier times women had learnt hand-sewing from the village glovemaking schools or from relatives. When the sewing machine was first introduced firms sent women out to show homeworkers how to use them. Some firms provided a training course in the factory for girls who had just left school. Clementina Black's pre-First World War enquiry recorded four widows, all over fifty years of age, earning on average four shillings or five shillings a week making gloves at home.[13] One respondent reported that his grandmother was making gloves throughout the 1870s for 3¼d. per pair.

The chief areas of the hosiery industry were the midlands counties of Nottinghamshire, Derbyshire and Leicestershire. Hosiery manufacture involved making stockings, socks, undershirts, drawers, gloves and jackets. The Children's Employment Commission of 1863 reported that much hosiery work was still conducted in private houses and small shops. The homework included chevroning stockings or socks, herring-boning the necks of vests or putting a silk flap on to the front, button-holing and much seaming (joining the parts of a garment together).

The chevroning or embroidering of fancy socks or stockings was one of the most skilled forms of hosiery work. A pattern of hose was done inside the factory and then given out to the women to copy. One Nottingham respondent recalls her mother doing this chevroning. She was married to a handframe knitter and had worked at the chevroning before and after her marriage.

> They were given a design. A pattern of hose they called it one hose – or stocking – that somebody more experienced inside the factory had done was sent out and they'd give you a dozen – either stockings or socks, whichever it was, and you did it, most of it was in silk and you had to do five or six threads, it was so very fine and they had middlewomen to fetch it – well they used to send them hampers full of it and then the people like mother have to go to her and pick up what she could – she'd spread it out amongst as many as she could, this lady. A dozen or two dozen . . . and you do all sorts of patterns. I've done a dozen men's socks – that's twenty four in a dozen – for one and six a dozen . . . After a while you get very quick . . . I was fascinated, I was always watching her. She says, you're not going to do it. She says, you're pale-faced enough as it is, you want to run and play the same as other children. She always sat in the evenings – especially in the winter – they had gas lights you know and dad lit a globe like a goldfish bowl . . . Princess Mary's wedding – pure silk stockings for her wedding . . . this dear old lady who used to give the work out . . . came to mother's with this parcel, she said, I want you to be sure to put a clean white apron on when you do these . . . And she said – these are for Princess Mary . . . And she had to put H.R.H. – Her Royal Highness Princess Mary in cross stitching. And they were fine silk . . . Oh, but you know you couldn't tell a hand had touched them when she'd done them. And I really think she got a thrill out of it . . . each stocking she was doing it was rolled up in this white cloth – and she paid – I think double what she got for an ordinary job.[14]

The Children's Employment Commission estimated the total number of lacemakers in 1860 as 150 000, but as they pointed out, the numbers varied according to the season and state of trade.[15] The majority were the wives and daughters of agricultural labourers. Pillow-lace or hand-worked lace and machine-made lace formed the two branches of the lacemaking trade. Lace is an ornamental openwork fabric made by twisting or interlacing threads to make a pattern. Pillow or bobbin lace is a patterned fabric made by twisting and plaiting together the threads which are wound on bobbins.[16] These bobbins often had inscriptions on them and are now collectors items. According to the sensibilities of Thomas Wright, some of these inscriptions were rather 'naughty' one example of such being 'Kiss me quick my mother is coming'. 'But,' says Wright, 'if the preceding inscription is naughty, the following is worse still: "Don't tell my mother I love the boys" is decidedly brazen, while "I do so love the lads" is even worse; and one can only shake the head sadly at the frontless girl who wrote: "If I love the boys that is nothing to nobody". '[17]

Pillow lace takes its name from the round pillow placed on the knees of the lacemaker. A stiff parchment pattern was fixed on the pillow by pins and pins were used to prick out the pattern. The threads were wound on bobbins and twisted and crossed to make the lace. The pattern was made by weaving a thicker thread through the background lace.

Girls began to learn pillow-lace-making at special village lace schools from five years of age. Pillow lace was concentrated in two main districts: Honiton in Devon and the Midland counties. A great proportion of pillow lace was not made in the towns but in the villages. Dealers usually sold the materials, patterns and silks to the lacemakers. The finished lace was either sold to middle-women acting for dealers, or the lacemakers sold the lace on their own account. As one respondant recalls, standards were very high:

> Well (mother) was a lacemaker, she had to earn her living by lacemaking. Oh, she made some beautiful lace. My mother made lace for Queen Victoria. Yes, and it . . . was all colours . . . I used to have to take it to Bedford to a lacemakers . . . and it used to have beads on it . . . beads were worked in it . . . And there used to be lace buyers come round, and buy it. And it depended on how nice you did and how clean you kept it. Yes if it was at all discoloured in any way they wouldn't buy it. Then you'd got to sell it somewhere else, privately wherever you could.[18]

Lace-making involved sitting in a stooping position for hours on end, which resulted in back and neck ache. Poor lighting such as candlelight must have strained their eyes too when we remember the delicate and intricate nature of the work. The Children's Employment Commission made the following comments on the general state of health of the lacemakers:

> The general appearance of all regularly employed in lace work . . . is unhealthy. There is a general want of colour and also of animation . . . the worn and early-aged faces, and frequently the failing sight of those who have left warehouses and depend on taking work at their own homes or employing children, show unmistakeable marks of the labour that they have gone through, and the anxiety which they still suffer from the alternations of high pressure and absolute want of work.[19]

The cheaper, machine-made lace, instrumental in the decline of pillow lace, produced homework that no longer demanded any skill but was low-paid, tedious work. This was the case with the three main processes that were given out. First, 'clipping', which was cutting off the ends and knots of cotton left on the surface of the lace during manufacture; second. 'scalloping', which involved cutting out the shape of the lace at the edges; and third, 'drawing', which was pulling out the thread which held together the lengths of lace in a breadth or piece. Two subsidiary processes involved in the preparation of lace for sale were 'jennying' and 'spotting'. Jennying was winding the lace on to a card by means of a hand machine and spotting involved attaching little spots of chenille to veiling by means of a tiny wire in the chenille.[20]

Nottingham was the centre for machine-made lace. One respondent recalls.

> Every street nearly on St. Ansell Rd. district, you could see them doing their lacework on the front doorstep . . . they had – big bath tin, probably they used it for bathing in at the weekend, but as they drew these threads the lace would drop into this bath tin . . . the threads of the lace – as it was made on the machines . . . were always left on. Well you'd see these women with their small scissors, clipping, clipping . . . and then the scallopers . . . going round the scallops, trimming the lace off.[21]

Pillow lace did not require finishing, while finishing was the major component of the homework in the machine-made lace industry.

Competition from machine-made lace, and the Education Acts which resulted in the closing down of the lace schools, were the two most important factors involved in the decline of pillow lace. Thomas Wright also argued that around 1880 the wealthier classes were finding it impossible to obtain domestic servants. It was suggested that they should cease to buy pillow lace and force girls back into service. On the other hand, however, various philanthropists made attempts to form associations to protect the pillow lace industry. It is doubtful if either of these campaigns were important factors in influencing the state of the industry one way or the other. The census figures reflect the decline in pillow-lace-making during the second half of the nineteenth century. Whereas in 1851 there were 26 670 lace makers in the three East Midland counties, by 1891 there were only 3376.

Straw-plaiting was an important home industry in Buckinghamshire, Bedfordshire, Hertfordshire, Essex, Suffolk and Cambridgeshire. By 1851 nearly eighty per cent of the total work force (nearly 22 000) lived in the south east Midlands and over 10 000 of them in south Bedfordshire.[22] Lace-making and straw-plating both thrived in Buckinghamshire and Bedfordshire but in different districts of the two counties. Field work and agricultural gang labour for women was very rare in the plaiting districts. In 1861, 27 739 females were registered as employed in straw-plaiting. By 1871 the number was considerably higher, with 45 270 female straw-plaiters registered.

Straw plaiting was a rural skill and, as with the pillow lace, many children learnt to plait in special village schools. The women and girls prepared the straw for plaiting as well as making the plait itself. The wheat-straw was gathered and brought back to the cottage. It was then cut just below each joint and the 'stocking' drawn off. The straw was then bleached. This involved placing the straw in a wooden chest with a hot cinder in a saucer of brimstone placed in the centre. The lid was then closed and the brimstone left burning for two or three days. The straw had by this time been bleached very white. The straw was then split and the straws rolled to make them soft. They were then ready to plait.[23]

One Essex woman rememberd the preparation of the straw and the making of the plait in her own home:

As a child I remember how the straw-plait was done in the home.

My mother used to walk about three miles to a farm, the Broad Farm, to buy a large bundle of straw that the farmer had picked out for making into plait. Then mother would clip it into short lengths and lie it in small bunches. Put it in a box with some brimstone and light it and close the box. This was called stoving it which would make it white. Then the straw would be split up with a small engine . . . then mother and my sister and brothers would start to make the plait. This was done in lengths of seventy yards then put on a board to straighten it out. There was a good many of these lengths made during the week. On Saturdays mother and all the neighbours would come to Wethersfield where a man would buy it to be made into hats but the plait is a thing of the past now. It was quite an Essex industry.[24]

The plaiters either sold to dealers who travelled from village to village or went to special markets where it was often possible to obtain a better price. In good times a woman could earn more at the plait than her husband or father earned working as an agricultural labourer. At times of agricultural depression or if a man was unable to do manual labour he might also turn his hand to the plait.

The straw plait was made into hats. Luton was the centre of the straw hat and bonnet trade. In the south Midlands hat sewers worked both in the factories and in their own homes. The supply of work was badly affected by season and fashion changes. A factory inspector estimated that a homeworker in the hat trade could earn twelve shillings by an average week's work and that she could hope for twenty weeks with full work, twenty-two weeks with some work and ten weeks with no work at all.[25] Felt-hat-making introduced in the 1870s did something towards relieving the slack season. The decline in straw-plaiting set in with the importation of cheap plait from China, Japan and Italy from the 1870s onwards and by the outbreak of the First World War the home industry of straw-plaiting had all but disappeared.

The homework trades so far considered have been in some way connected with the clothing industry. They were all important industries employing significant numbers of female homeworkers. The homework trades that follow, have been chosen as being representative of very different types of homework employment. They have been selected not only because some of them employed large numbers of homeworkers, but also because they give an idea of the wide variety of trades in which homework was an important factor of production.

Matchbox-makers and hook-and-eye carders were on the bottom rung of the homework ladder. They can been seen as the two homework trades which employd the least skilled and most destitute of homeworkers. In the nineteenth century, box-making factories were found in most English cities, but in particular, in London, the North West and the Midlands. A large variety of boxes were made to hold handkerchieves, buttons, shoes, bonnets, collars, ties, corsets, pills and medicine, soap, skittles, toys, candles, crayons, jewellery, wedding cakes, sweets, chocolates and, of course, matches.

It was a cheaper class of work which was most commonly given out to homeworkers. The box-maker in the factory was often a skilled worker. A girl could spend two years training on plain work and three years learning fancy work. This long apprenticeship may not have been necessary but it certainly legitimated paying low wages to 'trainee' factory workers. Nevertheless, fancy box-making required a certain amount of skill and training.

Matchbox-making was the branch of the trade which lent itself most easily to homework. It was unskilled work requiring no previous training. 'Industry not skill is the chief requisite, and 1½d. to 2d. an hour probably represents the amount that an average worker could earn if she worked hard and really wanted to earn her living.'[26] London was the centre of matchbox-making, with over one thousand women and girls employed in making matches in East London in the 1880s. Many matchbox-makers were the wives of dock labourers. The card for the boxes was cut out by the men in the factories. It was then fed through a machine which creased or scored the surface of the card along the lines where it had to be folded. The work given out consisted of folding and fastening the corners, covering the boxes and lids with paper and pasting on labels. During the process of matchbox-making each box had to pass eight times through the homeworker's hands.

Matchbox-making seems to have been a much-sought-after home industry, no doubt because it was an employment that anyone could do. This employment was popular which emphasises the lack of alternative work. Since the rates of pay were very poor. The Women's Industrial Council survey of thirty-five home industries in London in the 1890s concluded:

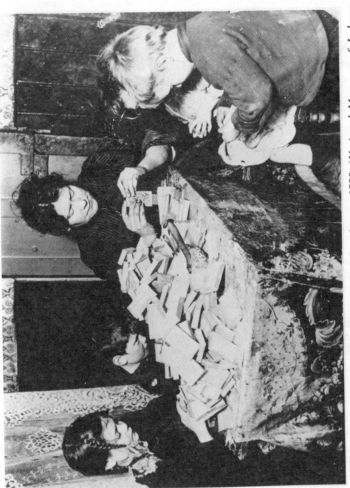

8 Matchbox-making in the East End of London c. 1890 (*National Museum of Labour History*)

A careful examination of the whole collection of facts leads to the conclusion that matchbox making is the home trade which appears to unite the greatest number of disadvantageous features (although it is not a markedly irregular trade), and probably the worst paid upon the whole of any industry here dealt with.[27]

Hook-and-eye carding was the major unskilled home industry in Birmingham. Hooks and eyes, buttons and safety pins were all carded by homeworkers. Will Thorne, born in Birmingham in 1857, records in *My Life's Battles* the role hook-and-eye carding played in his family. He was only seven and the eldest of four children when his father died:

> Our poverty compelled my mother to take any work she could get. She made a contract with a manufacturer of hooks and eyes to sew these small articles on thin cards. There were twelve hooks and twelve eyes to be sewn on each card, and the payment for this work was 1½d. per gross of cards, and my mother had to find her own needles and cotton. My elder sister used to help her, as well as looking after the two younger sisters. It was here I had intimate experience with sweated labour.[28]

Rates of pay varied from 9d to 1s. 4d. per pack. A pack usually consisted of two dozen gross of hooks and eyes. The cost of the cotton the homeworker had to provide was estimated at about one penny in the shilling and needles about one farthing per week. Average earnings of hook-and-eye carders were around 3s. 3½d. per week.[29] The work was commonly given out by middlemen. The only point in its favour seems to have been the fact that the supply of work was fairly regular.

Chain-making and nail-making were unusual home industries in that in no way could they be construed as more acceptable occupations for women than factory or field work. The work was manual and therefore by defination 'unwomanly'. Nail and chain-making were Midland industries. Nail-making was concentrated in Bromsgrove and Dudley while chain-making was centred in Cradley Heath.

It was common practice in nail-making for a girl and a man to work together in a domestic forge. The iron needed to make the spike nails was supplied to the workers in bundles of rods 56lb in

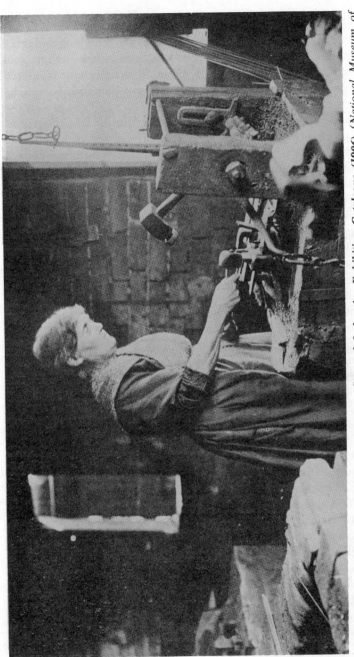

9 Homeworker at anvil in forge. Daily News Sweated Industries Exhibition Catalogue (1906) (National Museum of Labour History)

weight. The workers had either to collect the iron themselves or pay for its carriage. A spike nail was about eight inches long and three quarters of an inch thick. The rod was first cut into the requisite lengths by means of the oliver (a spring-tilt hammer which required a great deal of strength to operate and was therefore potentially dangerous) fixed to the block upon which the anvil was placed and worked by a sort of treadle. The man placed the rod on a chisel fixed in a block by the side of the anvil. The girl then stood close behind the man, holding him by the waist, and together they jumped on the treadle which worked the oliver. Of course this physical contact between the sexes was abhorrent to respectable society.

The man then took a number of short lengths of rod and plunged them into the fire. When the iron was heated he removed one piece, dropped the cold end into the socket of a tool and, using the hand-hammer and the oliver in rapid succession, formed the head. It was then flung across to the girl who had to make the spike. She plunged the cold end into the fire and as soon as it was heated used the hand-hammer and oliver until she had shaped the iron to a point. Needless to say the work demanded a great deal of physical strength from the women workers. The nails were often sold via a middleman, or 'fogger' as he was known in the trade. The Select Committee on the Sweating system in 1889 found a husband and wife earning only ten to seventeen shillings between them in a busy week and also nail-making was irregular work.

All kinds of chains were made by men and women in the Cradley Heath area. The women worked in tiny sheds, sometimes alone and sometimes with two or three other women. Each shed was equipped with a bellows on the left of the forge, and anvil, hammer and pincers. The chains were forged link by link using sheer strength and skill. The work was physically very demanding and working conditions exceedingly unpleasant.

The majority of female chain-makers were widows or wives and daughters of chain-makers and miners. Their children could be found playing around the mother while she worked or even helping in the forge itself. It was not unusual to see a baby being rocked to sleep on the top of a pair of bellows. Rates of pay were exceptionally low in a trade where a twelve-hour working day was more the norm than the exception. In 1900, women chain-makers were receiving on average only about 5s. 6d a week. The hard physical nature of the work and the squalid workshops appalled visitors to the area.[30] The

Daily News estimated that at the time of the 1910 strike about 1300 women were working as chain-makers.[31]

This chapter does not attempt to provide an exhaustive list of all the home industries carried on in England during the period 1850–1914. However, the above examples illustrate the wide range of industries that have made use of home labour and the multitude of different work processes to which women turned their hand in the hidden workplace of their own homes. During our research for this book we uncovered many more home industries which are to numerous to mention, many being specific to a particular locality.

5

The tailoring industry, 1850–1914

A detailed study of the tailoring industry is particularly appropriate in relation to homework since the industry employed many women in their homes in most of the tailoring centres in the country. Tailoring had a rigid sexual division of labour based on differentials of strength and skill and the position of women in the badly-paid sectors of the industry remained unchanged with the introduction of machinery to the industry. Women could buy or rent sewing machines and use them in their homes. The expansion in demand for ready-made clothing in the early twentieth century was not met by improvements in technology but by employing more women as homeworkers. The numbers of women homeworkers as a proportion of the total work-force in tailoring varied according to where the industry was situated. In this chapter, the effects of the introduction of the sewing machine in tailoring will be discussed. This is followed by a comparison of three geographical areas where tailoring was carried out in the late nineteenth and early twentieth centuries.

The invention of the sewing machine resulted in great numbers of women and girls continuing a process that had begun in the 1820s and 1830s. The wages of craftsmen tended to fall as a result of this and the monopoly of male labour in the industry was largely destroyed, but this had substantially occurred before the sewing machine came into widespread use. Work was concentrated in factories in some areas of the country but the picture is complicated and many work processes continued to be undertaken by homeworkers. From the last decades of the nineteenth century, as sewing machines became cheaper and it became possible to buy them on hire purchase or second-hand from factories, the homeworkers began to own their own machines and the sewing machine transformed the households of the homeworkers into miniature sweatshops. The mothers ran the machines while the children sewed on buttons and stitched hems. The long-term effect of the invention of the sewing machine upon women working in tailoring is summed up by Joan Scott:

> Scholars who have examined the experience of women in industrial society have concluded that such innovations as the spinning-jenny, the sewing machine, the typewriter, the telephone, the vacuum cleaner and the computer have not fundamentally changed the economic position of women or the prevailing evaluation of women's work. Dramatic technological changes did not result in equally dramatic social changes . . . on the contrary mechanisation has served to reinforce the traditional position of women both in the labour market and in the home.

The sewing machine increased the speed with which goods could be sewn, standardised the products and perhaps created more jobs. The machine did not, however, alter the low rates of pay nor the fact that large numbers of married women continued to be employed as homeworkers. Thus the mechanisation of homeworking did not free working-class women from the household; instead the sewing machine was incorporated into the traditional pattern of work at home.

Machinery does not develop in an ideological and economic vacuum. It is no accident that some machines are too heavy for women to operate or said to require too much skill. The sewing Machine, like the typewriter in the twentieth century, was developed in such a way that women could use it because, first sewing has traditionally been an occupation suited to women as it fits in with their domestic role; and second, women workers were needed in the tailoring industry, primarily due to increases in demand which could not be met by a limited number of craft-conscious journeyman tailors. So mechanisation led to the proliferation of small producers and to a massive increase in homeworkers in some areas of the country.

68

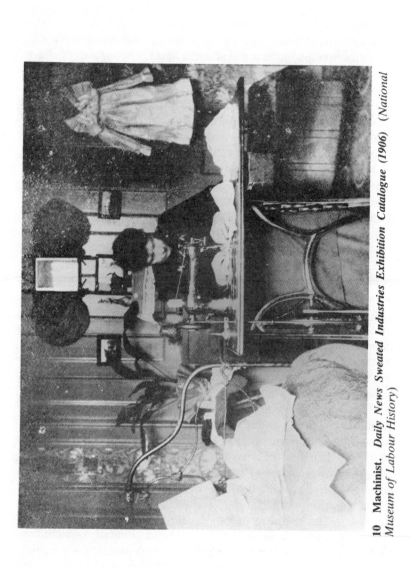

10 **Machinist.** *Daily News Sweated Industries Exhibition Catalogue (1906)* (*National Museum of Labour History*)

The number of homeworkers employed in the tailoring industry varied according to its geographical location: the industry became concentrated in a few areas of the country when it changed to a factory-based industry towards the end of the nineteenth century and tailoring centres began to emerge, and the most important factor which influenced where the clothing industry was situated was labour. The influence of the labour factor on the location of an industry depends on whether labour costs are a small or large proportion of the total costs of production. In clothing manufacture labour costs are an important part of the total costs of production, more important than the cost of capital equipment and allowance for depreciation. Because the area per worker is comparatively small, the cost of factory space is relatively slight.[2] In the manufacture of ready-made men's clothing, because it was based on mass-production techniques from the late nineteenth century onwards and not subject to the vagaries of fashion, labour costs constituted a smaller part of the total costs than in bespoke tailoring or in the manufacture of women's clothes. Therefore, the high index of labour costs in the tailoring industry meant that low labour costs in any given place exerted a strong attraction for clothing manufacture. The best place to locate a clothing factory would depend on the relative numbers of male and female workers required, the level of training required and whether the work could be done by young girls or boys.

Women formed a large proportion of the labour force in the tailoring industry and this proportion increased steadily from 1851 to 1911. Between 1891 and 1901 there was an increase in women workers in all areas of the country, ranging from 47.4 per cent in Manchester to 14.3 per cent in Norwich. However, between 1901 and 1911 the number of women workers decreased in some areas, especially in East Anglia where they had fallen by 17.5 per cent in Essex (mainly in Colchester) and 20.9 per cent in Norwich. In the more prosperous northern areas of Manchester and Leeds, they had grown by 7.2 percent and 13.4 per cent respectively.

The availability of female labour was much more important than male. The ease with which the industry could attract women workers depended on the population of the area concerned, but it also depended on what jobs were available for men, the wages they were paid and the alternatives for women in the area. The industry also needed a plentiful supply of girl workers who could be paid very little while training, were easy to train and tended to be faster workers. Because training machinists was not lengthy or difficult, no previous skills were necessary for women entering the industry. In fact, all girls in the nineteenth and early twentieth centuries learned needlework at school and would have had some experience of sewing, if not of machining. It follows from the above, then that the clothing industry would optimally be located in areas with a cheap supply of female labour, especially young girls, with few alternatives open to them.

In the tailoring industry, as in others, great local variations in women's wages were found. There was no general rate for the industry, only a general rate for the locality.[3] Assuming the female labour force to be highly immobile, the local rate of wages in any particular industry depends more than anything else upon the rates paid in other industries offering alternative employment.

Undoubtedly it was the textile industries of the North which kept up the rates of women's wages in the clothing industries of Leeds and Manchester. In Bristol, Colchester and Norwich, where opportunities for women were few, the young girls, entering clothing factories had no defence against low wages. The lowest wages in the country for women workers were in Bristol (11/10d. a week), followed by London (11/11d.), Essex (12/8d.) and Manchester (13/7d.). The highest wages were found in Leeds (13/8d.). These figures are for full-time workers only and do not include homeworkers. The figure would be far lower especially in Bristol, Essex and Norwich if homeworkers wages were included in the average.

In the East End of London, families had to depend on casual earnings. Low wage districts attempted to defend their position with the argument that Leeds and Manchester were far more favourably situated for sources of supply, coal and markets than were the southern countries, but by the end of the nineteenth century there was no truth in this contention. The supply prices of materials were standardised and London was as good a market as northern industrial areas. It could be that in the early pioneering days, the relatively favourable situations of Leeds and Manchester permitted fair wages and that local wage variations for women were partly determined by local custom.

To take advantage of the cheap supply of female labour, work was often cut out on the employers' premises in London and was made up by homeworkers in the provinces. A. J. Hollingtons of Aldgate were an example of this process. A representative of Hollingtons wholesale house, which produced clothes for export to the colonies, told the Select Committee of the House of Lords on the Sweating Systems of 1888 that the firm had sixty to seventy men on the premises who cut out garments by hand and machine and that the making-up was done outside by contractors: 'I have not the slightest idea how many are employed', he confessed. A third of the work given out by this firm went to garrison towns and agricultural districts in Hampshire and Essex, where the work was made up by the wives and daughters of soldiers and agricultural workers.[4] In and around certain towns in non-industrial areas of the South, for example Colchester, Plymouth and Bristol, women homeworkers continued up to the First World War and beyond. In the North, the wholesale manufacture of men's clothing became increasingly concentrated in Leeds where it was carried on in large factories with the aid of steam power.

Why did homeworkers in tailoring form 3.5 per cent of all women workers in Leeds, 11.4 per cent in London and at least 37.9 per cent in Colchester in 1911? R. H. Tawney suggests that the reason for the difference in the proportion of homeworkers in different areas is that homework flourishes where men's wages are low or their employment irregular and where there are few alternative occupations open to women. Tawney continues:

> It is, in short, not an indispensable part of the tailoring industry without which other branches could not be carried on but a development into which employers deviate in those districts whose peculiar economic conditions make large numbers of married women anxious to supplement their husbands' earnings by working at home.[5]

This explains why the firms in the North of England who had adopted the most efficient machinery and organisation employed few homeworkers whereas in the South and East of England smaller factories with less up-to-date machinery relied on cheap and flexible labour in the form of homeworkers to make their profits.

In the late nineteenth and early twentieth centuries the tailoring industry came to be sited in the large centres of London, Leeds and Manchester, although smaller clothing centres remained, especially in East Anglia (Norwich and Colchester) and the South-West (Bristol). Different sorts of clothing were made in different centres. In Leeds, mainly outer clothing was made, usually of wool; Halifax and Huddersfield made primarily cords and moleskins. Raincoat manufacture was concentrated in and around Manchester and there were miscellaneous clothing trades in the West Midlands, the Bristol area, South Wales and around Nottingham. The Eastern counties, especially Norwich and Colchester, were leading centres for tropical wear. In London, the West End had bespoke tailors catering for a wealthy clientele whilst the East End tailoring centres were engaged in every branch of tailoring. Ninety per cent of clothing workers were found in these areas.[6]

Comparison of three tailoring areas – Leeds, the East End of London, and Colchester – illustrates the differences between areas. Leeds is situated in a northern industrial area; wages for men were relatively high and there were opportunities for women to work in other industries. The tailoring industry in this area had large factories with a degree of unionisation and comparatively high wages for tailoresses. In the East End of London, the men were employed mainly as dockers on a casual basis. In this area, the tailoring industry was organised around small workshops with some homeworking. Thirdly Colchester was a small market and garrison town set in a rural area where the men were employed mainly as small builders or casual labourers in the town, and as sailors or agricultural labourers in the surrounding villages. The wages of men in this area were generally too low to support their families. Tailoring in Colchester was carried out in small factories in the town with large numbers of married women employed as home-workers in the surrounding villages. However, it is argued that although there were some differences between the geographical areas in terms of the structure of the industry, the sexual division of labour was similar in all three places. Wherever they worked, women were constrained in terms of the jobs they did and the wages they received by material and ideological factors relating to their gender.

The tailoring industry in the East End of London was organised along two distinct lines. On one side was the Jewish contractor, primarily involved in coat-making,[7] with a highly organised staff of fellers, machinists, buttonhole hands and pressers together with a mass of English women unorganised and unregulated and working in the lower sections of the trade. This system was what was known as the 'sweating system'.[8] On the other side were the English tailors with regulated pay and restricted hours working on the old traditional lines of one man, one garment. Waistcoats were largely made by women, and hand-sewn trousers by men. Women were in competition with German tailors for the manufacture of machine-made trousers.

The women in the lowest branch of tailoring in the East End worked either directly for a wholesale house or for a distributing contractor. They were German or English women, or more rarely Jews, as Jewish women seldom worked after marriage. Some were the wives and daughters of dockers and others in similarly precarious occupations in the East End, and many were widows. The problem of the low wages of these women arose from the seasonal and highly competitive nature of the tailoring industry from its low productivity and the prevalence of homeworkers.[9]

In summary, the amount of money women could expect in this period varied according to whether they were married or unmarried, what their husbands' did and where they lived.

———

With regard to the regularity of work, conditions in Leeds were better than those in other parts of the country. There were larger units of production which were less dependent on individual orders; the Leeds clothing trade was never the fashion trade to the extent it was in London. Moreover, with larger units of production and fewer homeworkers, trade union organisaton was stronger and able to insist on greater regularity of employment. Wages were also higher in Leeds than in the South, and Leeds did not have the extensive system of homeworking which was the worst feature of the industry in the South. The number of wholesale clothing firms grew from 21 in 1881 to 145 in 1911. In the 1880s Leeds surpassed her chief rivals in absolute numbers of both male and female operatives. The Leeds share of the national tailoring workforce increased throughout the period 1880 – 1914 in contrast with London, Bristol and Manchester. In Leeds, the increase was from 3 per cent in 1881 to over 9 per cent in 1911, whereas the other centres stagnated.[10]

The wage issue was complicated by the presence of homewor-kers. In Leeds, where the scale of production was greatest, the employment of homeworkers provided the most startling contrasts in scale and conditions. During the expansion of the 1880s, only one wholesale house did not employ homeworkers. In 1902, the first year for which such information became available, the Leeds total was reported as 500 and by 1904 a figure of 1100 was returned by the Chief Inspector of Factories, this was the apparent result of increased efficiency in the gathering of information.[11] However, the factory inspectors relied on the lists of outworkers supplied by the employing firms under the 1895 Act. If lists were not supplied there was little that the inspectors could do, provided that more homeworkers were employed than returned.

The system of homeworking, as we have seen, was not as widespread in Leeds as, for example, in Bristol, London or Colchester. In Bristol and Colchester the tailoring outworkers were much more numerous than in Leeds and they formed an integral and permanent branch of the trade. In Leeds, the homeworker was regarded as an 'economy of growth' by the large firm. The homeworkers' role in Leeds was transient and auxiliary and this partly explains the relative freedom of the town from national criticism on this score. Moreover, the actual numbers of homeworkers declined between the 1870s and 1890s. However, homeworkers were still employed until 1914 in numbers sufficient to generate grievances and to cloud the idyllic picture often painted of the Leeds clothing industry.

The low earnings of tailoresses in the Colchester area were caused by the general industrial character of the district.[13] In this area, the men's wages were low. The conditions for men in the area – the lack of industrial employment, especially when the shoe-making factories closed in the late nineteenth century – and low agricultural wages, meant that women were obliged to work for what pay they could get: 'The disorganisation of low rates of one industry spreads like an infection to industries apparently quite unconnected with it.'[14]

Union activity among male workers in Colchester tended to fluctuate with the economic situation, both local and national. There were virtually no large trade unions in Colchester until the late nineteenth century. The unions set up in the town after 1863 were small, craft-based, non-militant unions of the 'New Model' type. Only after 1892 did trade unionsm emerge on a large scale and it was to decline again after 1895 with high unemployment. The labour movement in the town did not revive until 1910. As the position of women workers was linked with that of the male work-force, the intermittent and generally low level of trade union activity among men was a factor militating against women joining and becoming active in trade unions, either with men or on their own behalf.

Some of the tailoresses in the Colchester area lived and worked in the town itself but many homeworkers lived in the surroundng villages. There were very few employment possibilities for women in this area. The numbers of women employed on the land declined in the last half of the nineteenth century and coupled with the decline in agricultural employment for women was the decay of the rural home industries such as lace-making and straw-plaiting.[15] Thus in the late nineteenth and early twentieth centuries, Essex women were rarely employed on the land except for some seasonal work. Rural industries had declined and male farm labourers were amongst the lowest paid in the country. There was a readily available pool of women, geographically immobile, confined to the home by domestic responsibilities and anxious to earn money. The tailoring industry was swift to take advantage of this situation. In the coastal villages, married women also needed to earn money because their husbands were sailors and fisherman and the work was seasonal. Whatever, they earned during the summer yachting season had to be used carefully to help keep their families during the winter, when money was scarce.

It was suggested by Mrs. Pat Green, a local Fabian, in 1912 that the rural and urban workers in the tailoring industry were handicapped by the cheap price at which wives in the yachting districts accepted work in order to occupy their time while the husbands were away. She said that they worked for 'pin money' and that the district was renowned for the smart dresses among the women.[16] Clementina Black carried out some research in Rowhedge for her book, *Married Women's Work*. She found that an average worker employed by an averagely paying firm and working from after breakfast until teatime would appear to earn about 7s. a week. But the difference between one employer and another were great.[17] Black also suggests that the wives in the yachting districts worked for pin money: 'With her own earnings, she is able to buy what she wants, pretty clothes for her children or for herself, a bicycle, a piano . . .'

However, the homeworker tell a different story. A witness before a public inquiry in 1912, a homeworker from Brightlingsea employed by Hart and Levy's, said she depended on the work for a living. She worked from nine in the morning until nine at night and in a busy period she earned between 25s. and 25/6d. a day, but when the work was slack only 4s. a week. Another witness from Brightlingsea said her husband was a yachtsman and his work only lasted about three or four months out of the year and she worked to keep her children. She did not work for 'pin money'. Her earnings were scarcely ever more than 5s. a week and she worked through the afternoon and evening.[18]

Women interviewed in Rowhedge also spoke of the money earned by taking in tailoring as being necessary for the welfare of their families. They said that the wages of their fathers and husbands were never enough to support the whole family (see chapter 2). Although the wages of the men employed on the yachts were higher than those of the agricultural labourers in the area, their work was seasonal and unreliable. They did not always get work on the yachts and their earnings during the winter months were also uncertain. Fishermen were usually self-employed and their earnings depended on what they could catch and sell. Therefore their wives also needed to earn money and took in tailoring at home from the Colchester factories.

In Colchester tailoring started in a small way in the 1850s. Then in the 1860s a succession of London firms began to establish branches in the town to take advantage of the cheap labour available both in the villages and among the fast-growing female population of Colchester. With the closure of the silk mills, only domestic service and a small amount of shop work offered alternative employment. It was estimated by the Select Committee of the House of Lords on the Sweating System (1890) that labour was half the price in the provinces than it was in London:

(Chairman)*Why is it you say that work can be done in the provinces that in London?*
(Mr. Moses, tailor) I suppose they can live cheaper; rent is cheaper and it is all female labour.
And do you think that female labour is paid less highly in the provinces than it is in the East End of London?
Unqestionably, by half

. . . Iam not alluding to provincial towns such as Manchester or Liverpool. I am speaking of provincial towns where factories are established.
Such as Leeds and Stroud?
Yes and Colchester; such places.[19]

Messrs H. E. and M. Moses employed Colchester women in their own homes, sending work down from London until they opened a factory in Colchester with 180 women machinists. Hammonds began in 1854 and by 1871 had 500 employees, including homeworkers. Altogether there were six large firms in 1865, giving work to 2500 women and girls and 200 men.[20]

By 1900, 1500 girls were employed in factories in Colchester. This was only a small part of those actually employed in the tailoring industry since most firms sent cut-out garments to be made up in the surrounding villages up to a distance of about ten miles. Most were taken by carriers' carts – there were about sixty running every week between Colchester and places in the vicinity – and the finished garments were brought back by the same means. Carriers received money from the workers which was spent on groceries to be taken back out to the village.[21]

Hyams remained the largest firm, employing 300 workers in Colchester and sending work by motor car to North Essex Villages. Hammonds, renamed the Colchester Manufacturing Company (also known as Turners), continued in Stanwell Street with over 1000 employees working at home and in the factory. In 1902 they installed electric power from Paxman-driven generators to work sixty sewing machines. In the First World War the company founded branch factories at Brightlingsea and Rowhedge. The business was linked with Vincey's in London which specialised in tropical suits (which were exported to South Africa) and overalls, and jackets which waiters wore on the railways. Canon Turner remembered that when his father left school and joined CMC, in about 1900 one of his jobs was to cycle round the villages and visit the women in their homes. The factory supplied them with their treadle machines. He also used to go round with a van-first horse-drawn and then a motor van. He would take round the cut-out bundles and payment for the last week's work. Canon Turner remembered that:

The homeworkers usually had families and needed the money, they were not able to come into the factory even when there was public transport. I used to go round in the van myself, as a child. All the materials and the machine were provided by the firm. The women could buy the machines at a reduced rate or, if not, it would come back to the factory when they finished work.

In the factory there were treadle machines first then power machines in long rows. I remember the steam so I think they were steam operated. Men did the cutting and always wore caps. The odd bits of material were known as fents. I used to ask for bundles of fents and people in the parish used to make things for bazaars with them.[22]

The cause of Colchester tailoresses, was taken up spasmodically by individuals with a social conscience, for example, by Liberal and Fabian women, Pat Green and Clementina Black and by the Colchester Trades Council. There was a strong feeling that Colchester tailoring was a sweated industry. The solution to the problem was seen to be the organisation of tailoresses into trade unions. This was suggested over and over again with no real results until the First World War and was based on a lack of insight into the particular problems faced by women workers. Those concerned with improving their position usually tried to organise them on the same basis as male workers as if the two were equivalent.

There were a number of basic problems involved in the organisation of tailoresses in the Colchester area. First, the area was one of low pay for men, furthermore, low industrialisation and lack of class consciousness had led to poor organisation among male workers. Second, the structure of the tailoring industry in Colchester was one of small family firms where the women owed or felt they owed a personal loyalty to the employer. In Turner's factory, for example, the employer would be called Mr Sydney or Mr Harold and would walk round the factory talking to the workers and go to visit the homeworkers in their cottages and any hostility was likely to be directed towards the foreman rather than the employer. Such personal loyalty militated against the formation of solidarity based on common class perceptions. Moreover, the structure of the tailoring industry which was divided into factories, workshops and homeworkers meant a lack of spatial and psychological cohesiveness among its workers.

As regards working conditions, the Factory and Workshops Act of 1893 required that occupiers of every factory or workshop manufacturing clothing or other articles, and all contractors employed by the occupiers, should keep a list showing the names of every person employed by him on his premises or working at home, and the places where they were employed. Every list should be open to inspection by the Factory Inspectorate. H. M. Inspector for Colchester reported in March 1883 that progress had been made toward complying with the order and that lists of outworkers employed in the principal tailoring and boot and shoe factories had been made. There were 2090 people on the list for tailoring, about 800 of whom were employed in Colchester and the remainder in the villages within a circuit of 10-12 miles.

Mr Wicks of the Sanitary Committee of Colchester said that the Home Secretary's order under the above Act had been made because of a statement in the House of Commons that Prince George of Wales had had his clothes made in a house in which typhoid fever was prevalent. The Sanitary Committee had been informd by several of its members that they knew of cases in Colchester where 'poor creatures suffering from typhoid and other fevers were at night covered up with the garments which they had taken home to make'. The Council was urged to take steps for the inspection of outdoor workers' workshops,[23] One wonders whether the concern expressed was for the workers with typhoid or for the possibility that the Royal recipients of the clothing might contract the disease.

At a meeting of the Ipswich and Colchester Trades Council in November 1883 the attitude of male unionists was clear: a Mr Dent argued that the practice of doing tailoring work in private homes should be stopped. 'It might be hard upon some married women,' he said, 'but they ought not to be expected to earn wages. If men could not keep wives they ought not to marry them.'[24]

In the years immediately preceding the First World War, about a dozen firms and contractors in Colchester were still giving work out to women in surrounding villages:

Well, lots of the women after they'd married used to do the same work at home . . . the money was shocking. But it was all sweated labour, 'course they didn't look on it as that because, well, they'd always been used to it you see. 'Course they married and they could do that at home and look after their children as well, you see. The great snag was that they had to go and fetch this work from the factories and take it back . . . they used to have to push these bundles on prams or carry them or if there were big children, the big children would have to take them . . . I did it myself for a woman who was getting elderly . . . and of course the money was shocking really, but there again you see people were glad to earn . . . and the work for women was very limited.[25]

Piece work rates paid by the Colchester tailoring firms ranged from 3d., for a pair of trousers in the late nineteenth century to 2s. before the First World War:

How much do you think you and your mother could earn in an average sort of week?
Well . . . if it was two shillings in the old money a pair we used to think that was good. I have made them for eighteen pence.

They brought it here by cart and they hired a room, and the women had to take the work in to be passed. The rate for ordinary work was 3d. a pair. The person who had the machine had the 3d. She did the machining then she would pass the work on to the people who did the handwork. They had to sew the bands in, do the flies and sew the buttons and the button holes and do the turn-ups and they got half, they got three ha'pence. That was accepted. But the whites was 4d. and the people who did those were very special people . . .

Each machine would be supplying three or four other women.

How many pairs of trousers do you thinks your grandmother used to do a week?
Oh well, they would want to do two or three pairs a day.

These women were mainly engaged in plain machining:

I used to make thirty pairs of trousers a week. They were all cut out ready. 'Course you had to make 'em properly. Sit down at the machine and put them together you might well say. They used to do all the sewing part in the factory, you see.

The comparison between Colchester, Leeds and the East End of London demonstrate that the tailoring industries had some common features, but also differed according to the area. All three areas employed a high proportion of women workers and they were always excluded from the most lucrative sectors of the industry such as cutting and pressing. The most marked difference between the Colchester industry and the others was its lack of Jewish labour. Jewish immigrants were blamed for the low wages and sweating system of the East End of London and for the problems of the Leeds tailoring industry. However, the wages of tailoresses in Colchester were among the lowest in the country – certainly lower than those in Leeds. This must suggest that the explanation for tailoring becoming a sweated industry lies elsewhere. It is more likely that the low wages of tailoresses were related to the wages and employment position of men in the area they came from. They were also related to the alternative occupation available to women and to the prevailing ideology about married women working.

The textile industries of the North kept up the rates of women's wages in the clothing industry of Leeds. Moreover, there was a tradition of married women working in factories in that area which dated from the early years of the Industrial Revolution. On the other hand, the married women of the Colchester area had a few alternative employment opportunities and were forced on to the labour market because of their husbands' meagre wages. In the East End of London the casual nature of the work available to men, in particular dock work, made it imperative for their wives to earn money wherever they could.

Trade unionism was rather more successful in Leeds than in the other areas. The Industry was organised on a large scale and women workers congregrated in large numbers. This was not true of Colchester or the East End. Moreover, women working in the textile industry in the Leeds area had a tradition of unionism, but it still proved difficult to organise tailoresses, particularly home-workers, and this is related to the failure of unionism among women workers generally in the period.[26]

6

Homework as sweated labour

Homework exemplifies what we have come to understand by the term sweated labour. The intention here is to analyse the causes and conditions which were responsible for sweating in relation to homework, so it is important, therefore, to define the terms 'sweating' and 'sweated labour' and examine the various definitions put forward during the nineteenth century when the debate on sweating was at its height. It is not easy to give a succinct definition of the term but certain specific characteristics combine to create what we would today term sweated labour. Low pay, long hours and poor working conditions are the predominant characteristics of sweated labour and these often go hand-in-glove with unskilled labour, 'women's work', the absence of trade union representation and an ineffectual or negligible degree of statutory control. Sweated labour therefore involves a gross exploitation of a labour force by the employer. It involves a work relationship in which the balance of power is very much in the employer's favour. The 'sweating system' is a rather vague term which has been used to embrace a variety of different features typifying particular industries during the latter part of the nineteenth century. It was sometimes used to describe a peculiar form of industrial organisation, sometimes associated with a particular form of remuneration and sometimes with certain specific conditions of employment.

Interest in the sweating system developed as part of a growing general awareness and public concern about the problem of poverty. Charles Booth's study of poverty revealed the inequalities of sweating. He described the features of the sweating system in the East End of London in the 1880s:

By the general public the word has been readily accepted as meaning any employer whose workpeople are badly paid, harshly used, or ill provided with accommodation or any sub-contractor or middleman who squeezes a profit out of the labour of the poor.[1]

Booth suggested that it was not one system but 'many systems with which we have to deal each having its special faults'. The first system he described was one practised in the clothing trade in which the wholesale manufacturer employed a subcontractor or middleman/woman. This person collected the raw material from the manufacturer and distributed it among a number of workers to be made up, and made his or her profit out of the difference between the amount he or she has paid by the manufacturer and the amount they paid to the homeworker. This is the sweating system as it was applied to female homeworkers.[2]

The second definition of the term 'sweating' applied not so much to a system as to the character of the employer under the system. An employer who paid his worker so badly that he (or more usually she) was forced to work and live in poor conditions was defined as a 'sweater'. The third definition, and the one which Booth himself was prepared to accept, was 'sweating' as 'expressing in a general way all the evils which the workers in certain trades or under certain conditions suffer'. So an examination of the 'sweating system' consists of looking at certain 'sweated industries' and the conditions under which employees worked. Each of these industries had its percentage of the very poor and its fringe of abject misery.[3]

In his summary Booth maintained that an inquiry into the sweating system must be 'an inquiry into certain evils which, though having no special connection with any particlar system of employment or caused by any particular form of tyranny, are none the less present and intensely so'. He attributed these evils to the 'multiplication of small masters and their tendency . . . to increase, owing to the smallness of the capital needed for commencing business in the so-called 'sweated' industries.[4]

The large numbers of foreign immigrants were seen by many as being responsible for introducing sweating. However, sweating existed prior to the large influx of Jewish immigration and occurred in many trades and areas of the country in which they did not predominate. The middleman or subcontractor was also commonly seen as being responsible for sweating. A great deal of poor quality work was given out at very low prices by subcontractors and they inevitably played a part of keeping wages below average. A system of subcontracting was to be found in many industries such as clothing, boot and shoe makeup, brick manufacture and mining. However, there was subcontracting without sweating just as there was sweating without subcontracting.[5] There is moreover, evidence that the very worst paid work of all was given out directly to homeworkers by wholesale firms. For example, the report given by Beatrice Potter to the Select Committee provides evidence to support this view:

> That work (lowest quality coats) is done by the men and women at their homes; it really does not pay the contractor to take it out. That is the sort of coat that is done for 7d. or 8d.; it hardly pays the Jewish contractor to take that coat out, so that it is done to a great extent by gentile women. That is the very lowest work; and that is what I mean by saying that sweating in its most intense form has nothing whatever to do with the contract system. In fact, the contract system is the top stratum, as it were, of the trade. It is taken straight from the wholesale houses. They earn the lowest wages in the coat trade.[6]

In 1888 a Conservative member of the House of Lords, Lord Dunraven, obtained from his colleagues the appointment of a committee to enquire into the sweating system. But the committee had 'no sooner begun its labour when it took flight'.[7] Lord Dunraven retired, his place was taken by Lord Derby, who had more moderate views and the committee's recommendations were very timid. The committee failed to put forward explanations for the existence of the sweating system but merely dismissed certain current explanations, claiming that it was not due only to middlemen and that foreign workers were not wholly responsible.[8] It was finally forced to conclude that one industrial system was always present in the sweated trades. 'Sweating' was defined as having unduly low rates of pay, excessive hours of labour and insanitary working conditions.

Several witnesses before the committee expressed the view that homework itself was an evil and should be eliminated. An extract of the interview with Lewis Lyons, journalist and tailor's machinist, illustrates this point:

(Earl of Onslow)
. . . Now do you mean to say that women trouser finishers or shirt finishers should not be allowed to take any work home to their own homes?
(Mr. Lewis Lyons (journalist and tailors machinist)
No they should not, that is the evil which I complain of.
(Earl of Onslow)
It is obvious that a married woman being at home with three children to take care of could not go out to do a day's work in the factory you propose should be set up but she gets work now at home, you would deprive her of the means of earning wages any more?
(Mr. Lewis Lyons)
If the husband earned sufficient money there would be no necessity for his wife going out to work.[29]

On the other hand, evidence given by Mrs Isabella Killick, a trouser finisher, demonstrates that not every woman had a man able or willing to support her:

(Chairman) *What business are you engaged in?*
On the trouser finishing. I have worked at it now about 22 years altogether; it is paid for now so terribly bad . . .
What do you earn a week?
I have to find my own materials; I cannot earn more than 1s. 2d. a day; and I have to find my own materials and fire and lighting out of it . . . I am up at six o'clock every morning and never done until eight at night.
Do you get about the same amount of work all year round
No, because it falls off at a certain time of the year; about two months before Christmas it falls off then it does not start again till a month after Christmas, about three months of the year is slack.
What do you do then?
I am glad to get anything to do, a bit of cleaning or washing; I cannot be without work as I have three little ones to support.[10]

Disclosures at the Select Committee of the House of Lords showed that far from being socially economical or useful, the industries carried out in the workers' homes were actually dragging back industry as a whole.[11] As a result of the Report of the Select

Committee and pressures from social reformers the idea arose that it might be necessary in the interests of public health to exercise stricter supervision over people employed in their homes who had previously been exempt from Factory and Workshop Acts.[12]

If it was difficult to determine the causes of sweating there was no such problem in indentifying the sweated labourers. Clementina Black and other active campaigners against the sweating system recognised that 'Homework, or at least an important part of that industry is in the odd situation of only surviving on account of its evils. Low pay and long hours are among the chief conditions of its existence.'[13]

> '(Sweating) is understood to mean that work is paid for at a rate which in the conditions under which many of the workers do it yields them an income which is quite insufficient to enable an adult person to obtain anything like proper food, clothing and house accomodation . . .[14]

The Select Committee on Homework provides a variety of reasons to account for the exceptionally low wages of homeworkers. First, sewing made up a large proportion of homework and as nearly all women could sew the supply of labour was always in excess of demand for it. Homework was very popular because it enabled women constrained by family commitments to bring in an income. The method of payment (that is, piece-rates) meant that those who were slow because of old age, poor health or lack of skill were still employable. Many homeworkers were in competition with machinery, they were unorganised and unable to resist employers' moves to lower rates in order to cut production costs.

Piece-work was recognised as a general characteristic of sweated industry and a salient factor in sweating:

> If it were possible entirely to abolish the piece work, work remuneration of all superintendents of labour, then, and then alone should we have got rid, root and branch, of the sweating system'.[15]

Piece-work can certainly be seen as a major element in sweating although not the sole cause. It is a useful system of payment for the employer and it is especially well suited to homework, which has always been exempted from legislation restricting the length of the working day. Payment by the piece gives the impression that the worker is paid an amount equivalent to the labour-power expended. Quick work produces more pieces than slow work, so piece-work gives the impression that the worker controls his or her earnings. In fact, the employer can still control the wages by alternating overwork with underemployment and he also determines the rate paid per piece. The piece-work system controls the quality and intensity of the labour and keeps the cost of supervision down to a minimum. It is a system that encourages the labourer to overwork. Payment by the piece also helps promote a system of subcontracting.

Another explanation for low wage rates is that the majority of homeworkers were women. Employers systematically paid women at lower rates even when they were performing similar tasks and producing similar quanitities of work to men. However, the employers' jobs were made easier by the concentration of women workers into certain sector of the economy such as homework.

Married women were seen by employers as subsidised workers willing to work for less than a living wage. This was a useful argument for any employer who felt the need to justify payment of low wages. The *Women's Trade Union Review*, the quarterly journal of the Women's Trade Union League, saw the married woman's attitude to work as having a detrimental effect on wage rates:

> In many instances the work of women is merely supplementary to that of their husbands, in which case they are not particular what wage they accept. This re-acts very hardly on those women who do entirely depend on their labour for their own subsistence and perhaps for that of their children.[16]

An article entitled 'High Ideals: Early Married Life, a paper for Working Women', published in *The Girl's Own Paper* in 1895, issued the following warning to readers:

> About you young wives taking in work at home instead of going out, may I say a few words? Do not work for too low wages just because you do not need high ones, not being entirely dependent on them, you help to lower the rate of wages, and so put obstacles

in the way of single women and widows earning enough for their living. Do you understand what I mean?[17]

Although maried women may have contributed to keeping wage rates low the evidence sometimes appears to be contradictory. For example, there were married women, who because they were not absolutely desperate, had stopped taking in work as it did not pay sufficient for the time and effort expended. Moreover, those 'found working at really starvation wages–sack makers and carpet slipper makers–were women who had either to support themselves or to fall back upon charity or the workhouse.'[18] R. H. Tawney's evidence also seems to support this view. He found that, in the case of tailoresses, those workers entirely dependent on their own earnings were lower paid than workers who were not.[19]

Wages paid for 'women's work' were glaringly inadequate. They resulted in hardship to the women themselves and also to their dependants. An itemised weekly expenditure for a shirtmaker and her child shows the poverty of an existence based on homework. The woman earned six shillings a week to keep herself and her child.[20]

Rent – one room	2s. 0d. a week
Tea ¼lb.	4d. a week
Sugar 2 lbs	3d. a week
Flour	1½d. a week
Oatmeal	1½d. a week
Margarine	3½d. a week
Six eggs (chipped)	3½d. a week
Ham	2½d a week
Coals	3d. a week
Onions, or other veg.	1½d. a week
Bread	4½d. a week
Kitchen costing about	3d. a week
Weekly total	4s. 9d.
Leaving 1s. 3d. for clothes and other expenses	

Thousands of homeworkers lived their lives on the very verge of starvation. Referring to the sack-makers, the Reverend R. C. Billing of Spitalfields, in his evidence to the Royal Commission on Housing reported that wages were:

(Rev.) Hardly sufficient for them to live upon. The misery of those who have to do work for shops of any kind is frightful.

(Chair) Do you know that it is dearer to make the sacks in any large quantity yourself than buy them? Taking into account finding the material and labour and all, the price that is paid is infinitely small . . .

(Rev.) It is not nearly sufficient to keep body and soul together.

(Chair) Does not it follow that the wretchedness and misery such as you have been witness of, is mainly the result of starvation wages which are paid to the people?

(Rev.) That is the case where the householder is entirely dependent upon this kind of labour.[21]

Inevitably, women having to support themselves and dependants were forced to look to ways of supplementing their earnings. Poor relief was necessary to supplement women's wages, although it was not always forthcoming. In 1902, H. Bosenquet examined the returns of the poor relief given during a period of three months to women in the East London union. The sample was one of 314 women receiving relief varying from 2s. to 2s. 6d. a week. A large proportion of the recipients were elderly, 275 being over sixty years of age and 69 of them over eighty years of age. Of the 275 over sixty years, the number presenting themselves as still earning was 246. The occupations of this group covered a large number of homework trades. Bosanquet found that the average earnings, from all the trades they were engaged in, was not more than three shillings a week.[22]

There was a general reluctance amongst the 'respectable poor' to claim poor relief and charitable assistance. For example, the Royal Commission on the Housing of the Working Classes reported the follow case of a widow:

(Rev. Smith) I have a woman in my Parish, a widow, with one child . . . and I have just got her a room in the Peabody Buildings. During the month of November she earned on an average 3s. 3d. per week; during the month of December she earned on the average 2s. 6d. per week; and during the month of January she earned 2s. 9d. per week . . .

(Chair)	Did she apply for outdoor relief?
(Rev.)	No she did not apply for out-door relief. She is a very respectable widow woman, and a woman who would not apply for out-door relief.
(Chair)	Was what she earned made by needlework?
(Rev.)	Yes by needlework, mantlemaking.[23]

Another important method of supplementing wages was prostitution. Mayhew had noted a high incidence of prostitution amongst needlewomen in the 1840s. 'There isn't one young girl as can get her living by slop-work', commented one needlewoman he interviewed, while another remarked, 'If I was never allowed to speak any more, it was the little money I got by my labour that led me to go wrong . . . But no one knows the temptations of us poor girls in want. Gentlefolks can never understand it.[24] Although Mayhew himself sometimes uses the term prostitution to mean cohabitation there can be no doubt that some homeworkers were forced to supplement their wages by going on the streets. The Select Committee on the Sweating System acknowledged the importance of prostitution as a casual occupation for women in the sweated trades.[25]

Irregularity of employment for both indoors and outdoor female hands was very high in trades such as tailoring and millinery. These workers were therefore highly represented amongst the casual prostitute population. Sweated labour with its abysmally low and irregular wages was a direct cause of the immorality the Victorian bourgeoisie so self-righteously condemned. In effect, the exalted position of the upper strata of society was achieved only through the economic moral and social prostitution of working-class women.

The majority of homeworkers could not afford to be particular about the rates they worked for. They had neither the time nor the money to travel from one employer to another in order to seek out the best rates. Their immobility confined them to a local market which in turn kept wages low and encouraged the growth of subcontractors. A uniformity or even approximate uniformity in earnings did not exist even within one trade: considerabe variations in rates of pay prevailed. However, comments about wage rates are frequently only comments based on the male working population and male-dominated industries and trades. This can present an inaccurate picture of the wage levels of an area. For example, in

London a large sector of the nineteenth-century working population were females working in poorly paid employments. Regional comparisons in wage rates are also complicated by regional variations in the cost of living.[26] A multitude of factors combine to make comparisons and generalisation about homeworkers' earnings an impossibility and one of the chief difficulties in the way of making an assessment of homeworkers' earnings is the irregularity and seasonality in supply of work.

The following tables taken from a blousemaker's wage book provide a rare and interesting piece of evidence of a homeworker's earnings. The wage book shows the figures for a whole year and provides a very clear example of the extent to which wages varied from week to week and month to month.[27]

	s. d.		s. d.		s. d.
January	10.4	February	13.2	March	12.7½
	5.9		17.1½		9.9
	13.7½		11.8½		17.0
	11.1		11.1		11.3
April	14.8	May	14.9	June	15.10½
	14.2		16.2½		5.10½
	8.3		8.9		12.10½
	7.6		11.6		8.7½
					6.5½
July	2.9	August	11.10½	Sept.	11.10½
	6.9		11.11		8.9
	10.9		12.3		no work
	12.3		7.6		
	11.3				
October	6.9	January	9.10		
	9.4		10.3		
	no work		11.7½		

For the woman who was the sole breadwinner seasonality and irregularity of production could only cause the greatest misery and hardship. There was a substantial amount of dovetailing between different occupations amongst the male casual work-force but this practice seems to have been much rarer amongst women.[28] East End female factory hands would often leave London for the fruit or hop-picking season. During slack periods in homework trades some women turned to cleaning or street selling. A number of the Black Country chainmakers went hop-picking. However, it was unusual for homeworkers to overcome the problem of seasonality by moving from one trade to another. The West Ham study noted only one case in which a woman carried on work in two trades with a summer and winter season respectively.[29]

Any information provided by employers of homeworkers has always been given reluctantly. The earnings registered by the employer in his book of outwork are also misleading in that they do not show how many hours the homeworker had to spend to earn a particular sum or how much help she had from neighbours or members of the family:

> The ordinary sack of course has to be sewn both sides, hemmed along the top, and they receive 1s. 7d per 100 for doing these; and it takes a skilled woman working long hours, two days to do 100 . . . The employers, if they were spoken to about it, would show you the book, against the woman's name, the amount received: but they do not say that the woman has, perhaps three or four children, and a neighbour's child working for her; that is where the falsity of the impression is when you see an employer's book of out-work.[30]

It was not until investigators went into the homes of the women and interviewed them that a more accurate account of their earnings became known. However, it still remained impossible to specify what the weekly earnings of a homeworker were in a situation where, for example, a blousemaker could earn seventeen shillings in one week, three shillings in another and for several weeks nothing at all. It was no solution to estimate the earnings per hour as the homeworker is subject to interruptions that do not trouble the factory worker. Her working hours are as variable as the rate of interruptions in each hour.

Many extra expenses also fell to the homeworker. Apart from having to foot the bill for expensive basics such as rent, heating and lighting, the homeworker was confronted by number of additional expenses incidental to each particular trade – oil, cotton, needles, string, paste or glue. In the clothing trade, a sewing machine was often required and this was the most expensive item of all.

Fines and deductions for late work played a part in cutting down wages even further. As the work was not supervised mistakes were more frequent than in the factory. The women were often forced to purchase the spoilt goods or redo the work free of charge. The West Ham study revealed a case in which a woman had one shilling deducted for a spoilt skirt which was, in fact, more than cost price. Fines were frequently imposed for late work.

This was a very unfair system as employers often used homeworkers to cope with surprise increases in demand. The fear of the consequences of not getting the work done on time drove many women to overwork themselves. This was, of course, an ideal situation for the employer, allowing him to cope with increases in demand without coming into conflict with the Factory Acts. Fines were also a more remunerative method of punishment than dismissal. Fines for lateness seem especially hypocritical when we know that workers were frequently kept waiting for long periods at the warehouses when they went to collect work. Fines and deductions were concealed ways of increasing the rate of exploitation. The absence of unionisation amongst homeworkers made them especially vulnerable to these sort of practices.

Almost without exceptions homeworkers' earnings were extremely low throughout the historical period 1850–1914 and the real wages of homeworkers experienced a decline during this time. This was to some extent due to increased competition between employers for contracts, and increasing competition with machinery. One homeworker recalled how nineteen years earlier she had received 2s. for the same amount of work for which in 1907 she was paid only 5d. Another worker stated that a shop which used to pay her 4s. a dozen sets of pillow-slips, paid her only 2s. in 1907.[31] A Mrs R also complained of lower rates. She had worked for forty years making coats and boys' reefer jackets. In 1907 she was receiving 2s. 6d. a dozen for coats and 2s. 3d a dozen for reefers, while ten years earlier she was paid 5s. a dozen from the middleman for just the same work. Eighteen years earlier she had been paid 1s, 1s.6d and 2s. a coat from the factory where all her work was done by machine, as it was in 1907.[32] Meyer and Black in their investigations at the beginning of this century claimed to have come across a number of cases in which payment was lower than it had been earlier while they found no cases in which payment for any particular kind of work had risen.[33] All the available evidence seems to point to a general decrease in the already sweated rates paid for homework during the latter nineteenth century and the earlier part of this century.

Inadequate housing and ignorance of basic health and sanitary provisions all contributed to the appalling 'sweated' working conditions of homeworkers. Improvements in sanitation, water supply, clothing, diet and education were necessary prerequisites to the eradication of those working conditions commonly associated with sweating. The major difference between the situation of homeworkers and the rest of the labour force is that the workplace of the former is the home. The female homeworker was therefore often wife, mother, housekeeper and breadwinner at one and the same time. The work routine of the homeworkers was complicated by the demands of family responsibilities:

> When the industrial work is carried on at home the worries and interruptions of family life must always contribute to the difficulty and intensity of the toil, and tell upon the nervous system and general health of the women workers.[34]

In contrast to the woman who went out to work, the homeworker had no change of environment and no companionship and conversation with workmates.

In the towns homeworkers were most frequently found living near to their own sources of work or close to the husbands' place of work. Evidence brought before the Royal Commission on Housing of the Working Classes revealed gross overcrowding in particular areas as a result of the need to live close to the source of employment:

> The mention of women and girls suggest another reason why certain localities are overcrowded. The subsidiary employment of wife and children has to be taken into consideration when the poor choose a place of residence. Whatever the contributions of these members of a family may be to the maintenance of the household, there is no doubt that the work of charwomen and sempstresses, and the labour in which children are employed, attract great numbers to the densely populated districts which provide such employment and away from the suburbs where such work would be out of reach.[35]

11 (& 12) Home and workplace! *Daily News Sweated Industries Exhibition Catalogue (1906) (National Museum of Labour History)*

12

Whenever possible homeworkers tried to live close to the warehouse so that they were aways readily available:

> There are those women who must take their work home, such as those who work for the city tailors: and the girls who are employed in small factories, such as those for artificial flowers; those also have to be in attendance morning after morning (like the dock labourers) whether there is work for them or not, for if they are not within calling distance, they lose it.[36]

Living close to the supply of work was also important because of the expense that could be incurred in travelling. For example, the Select Committee on Homework noted that at the beginning of this century the wife of an East End docker, doing homework, could spend eightpence in fares travelling three times a week in order to collect and return her work to the warehouse.[37] This was a significant sum when earnings were barely a few shillings a week. The 1907 West Ham study quotes two cases of shirt workers who were only allowed to earn a halfpenny on the work given out and had to return the work before they could take any more out.[38]

The rooms of the homeworkers were often already grossly overcrowded and the misery and squalor of poverty was accentuated where the home was forced to play the double role of both living and work space. Many contemporary reporters were no doubt guilty of too great an enthusiasm and willingness to criticise the living conditons and life-styles of the working classes and thus moral judgements were far more frequent than concrete and practical suggestions for improving the situation. Character defects such as idleness and moral degeneracy were commonly seen as the causes of poverty. Undoubtedly the great majority of homeworkers lived in terrible squalor and dire poverty. Specific economic causes forced homeworkers to live in conditions such as those of the fur-pullers described for us with a religious fervour in the emotive language of Edith Hogg:

> Here, in an endless network of pestilential courts and alleys, into which can penetrate no pure, purging breath of heaven, where the plants languish and die in the heavy air, and the very flies seem to lose the power of flight and creep and crawl in sickly, loathsome adhesion to mouldering walls and ceilings here,

without one glimpse of God's fair world, or of the worth and dignity of that human nature made after the image of the Divine, we find the miserably poverty-stricken rooms of the fur-pullers.[39]

The article was an effective propaganda piece in its day. It drew attention to one section of homeworkers and stimulated further investigation in this field. Fur-pulling in the home was eventually forbidden by law. The example of the fur-pullers perhaps shows the risk attached to working and living in the same room in its most intense form. The task of the fur-puller was to remove the long, coarse hairs from rabbits' skins. The pulled out hair was collected and weighed in the shop. The rooms of the fur-pullers were pervaded by the 'sickly, unmistakable smell of the uncleaned skins'. The windows had to be kept closed as any movement of air would only assist in forcing the lung hairs into the eyes, noses and lungs of the homeworkers; it was a trade closely associated with tuberculosis.

In a variety of other trades the homeworker and her family were subject to many adverse effects upon their health. Lack of ventilation, the failure to wear protective clothing in the form of overalls and caps while working, eating and sleeping in the same room in which a trade was carried on was detrimental to the health of many women and their families. The Royal Commission on the Housing of the Working Classes, did much to publicise the working conditions of homeworkers and drew attention to homework as a contributory factor to insanitary living conditions.

The model dwellings, for example the Peabody Dwellings, were intended to provide better housing for the working classes. However, their rules were such as to exclude a large number of the needy poor, for example widows and deserted wives. The model dwellings were in general out of reach of the strata of society with whom this study is concerned.[40] Certain homework trades were forbidden in these dwellings, for example fur-pulling, matchbox-making and other trades employing glue.

General overwork in unsanitary conditions and poor diet broke the strength of the women and weakened their resistence to illness. In rough trades such as sack-sewing and boot-sewing, the woman's hands were often damaged. One respondent recalls his mother's experience in the boot and shoe works:

I used to think it was terrible . . . I used to feel sorry . . . she would never say anything about it . . . Never heard her moan about how she was hard worked . . . With the cold weather in the wintertime, therefore you had to wax the thread, and the wax gets brittle in the cold weather you see. Well as you pull the thread it comes across your fingers. Cuts into the flesh . . . you have to pull it tight . . . it cuts the skin. And they don't heal because you're always at it . . . sore all the time. More like broken chilblains, that's what it feels like.[41]

The wretched wages of the homeworkers left no money spare for healing ointments or doctors' bills. The working conditions of many homeworkers were often not only a danger to themselves and their own families but also to the consumers of the goods they produced. If there was illness in the home of the worker shortage of space meant that the sick person could not be isolated and hence came into contact with the articles being made up in the home. Charles Kingsley, parson, author and sanitary reformer, wrote of this danger in 'Cheap Clothes and Nasty':

These wretched creatures, when they have pawned their own clothes and bedding, will use as substitutes the very garments they are making. So Lord –'s coat has been covering a group of children blotched with smallpox. The Rev. D– finds himself suddenly, unpresentable from a cutaneous desease which it is not polite to mention on the South of the Tweed, little dreaming that the shivering dirty being who made his coat had been sitting with his arms in the sleeves for warmth while he stitched at the tails. The charming Miss C– is swept off by typhus or scarlatina, and her parents talk about 'God's heavy judgement and visitation' – had they tracked the girl's new riding habit back to the stifling undrained hovel where it served as a blanket to the fever-stricken slop worker, they would have seen why God had visited them . . . [42]

The absence of inspection and any statutory requirements regarding hygiene and sanitary standards plus the abdication from any responsibility by employers made homework a powerful source for the spread of disease. The contrast between the high-class goods purchased by the consumer and the working and living conditions of the sweated homeworker is striking. For example, the following account is taken from an interview with a woman in the 1880s. Her work was to reline fur muffs and jackets for fashionable shops in Holborn. The interviewer noted that the woman was lining a sealskin jacket and expressed some surprise at finding that sweeping the floor was an integral part of the process:

> 'What are you going to do with that dust? well, you see I'm short of wadding, the woman said. They won't pay me till I take the work back, and I've not got any more wadding. If I go to the shop they'll say I was careless, so I'm just filling in with these sweepings;[43]

One isolated and localised philanthropic gesture which attempted to overcome the evils of working and living in the same room is interesting in that it shows clearly the utter failure of a certain sector of the population to understand the plight of working-class women. In 1894 a Mr W. H. Wilkins and a Reverend W. Davis opened a parochial Out-Workers Room in Bethnal Green and urged homeworkers 'to profit by its superior warmth, light and air'. A letter written by the latter gentleman shows the project to have been a failure:

> Our outworkers' room was closed last Saturday. It was so ill attended that I did not find myself justified in continuing it. A few women came, but very few. The experiment has once again proved the truth of what we so often feel – viz – that of all people, poor women are the most difficult to help, in as much as they will not play up to help themselves.[44]

The author of this letter seems rather offended that his philanthropic gesture should have been rejected in this way. His attitude reflects what was a widespread feeling amongst 'respectable' Victorian society: the poor were poor because they would not help themselves. There is no understanding here of why women did homework, as opposed to other types of employment. The majority of women were, of course, doing homework precisely because they were tied to their own homes and for a variety of reasons were not free to go out to work. It was no more likely that they could go to an outworkers' room than to a factory or workshop.

The provision of such services as outworkers' rooms was no solution to the sweated working conditions of the majority of homeworkers. Far-reaching and fundemental changes in society were needed to improve the conditions of existence of homeworkers. Few contemporaries were able to see, or indeed wished to see, the sweated conditions under which homeworkers were employed in the wider perspective which Beatrice Potter suggested.

> The mass of struggling men and women whose sufferings have been laid bare by the enquiry (Select Committee on the sweating systems) are oppressed and defrauded in every relation of life; by the man who sells or gives out material on which they labour, by the shopkeeper who sells them provisions on credit, or forces them under the truck system; by the landlord who exacts in return for the four walls of a bedroom or the unpaved and undrained backyard, the double rent of workshop and dwelling; and lastly, by every man, woman and child who consumes the product of their labour.[45]

It was in the trades where female labour was most prevalent that the three characteristics of sweating were most commonly found. As B. L. Hutchins wrote in her tract for the Fabian Society, the specific conditions of women's position in society made them the major reservoir for sweated industry:

> Sweated workers are sweated either because by reason of sex, age, infirmity or want of organisation and support, they have to let their work go cheap. They are compelled by need to sell their labour to the first purchaser who will take it, and cannot make conditions. They must work at the rates of pay the employer thinks good enough for them and the smallness of the pay automatically extends the hours.[46]

Although some of the worst home industries were banned as a result of the anti-sweating campaign at the turn of the century and although legislation was enacted in the form of the Factory and Workshops Act of 1901 and the Trade Boards Act, homework continued to be the sector of the economy which most exemplifies what we understand by the term 'sweating'.

7

Legislation and trade unions

The terrible conditions under which the majority of nineteenth-century homeworkers laboured were not as visible as those under which workers laboured in the factories or mines. It was not until the 1880s that the iniquities of the sweating system carried out in the homes of the workers became widely known to those outside the working class itself. This concern about homework must be seen against the background of the socio-political climate of the late nineteenth century. One of the most important issues of the 1880s was the poverty debate. Charles Booth's East End survey brought a new and more scientific approach to the study of poverty and coupled with this new investigative approach to poverty was a change in social attitudes. The 1880s also witnessed the growth of socialism and the development of the 'New Liberalism'. The women's movement, the trade union and labour movements and the settlement movement all made important contributions as pressure groups, so it became possible for a change in social thinking to develop. There was a shift of emphasis from individualism in social policy to greater pressure for state intervention and collective responsibility. Poverty was no longer seen to result purely from individual weakness of character, and specific environmental factors were isolated as causes of poverty.

Facts relating to wealth, land, industry, domestic issues, imperialism and poverty began to be systematically uncovered. These facts were disturbing – half the total national income went to one-ninth of the population; and half the national capital belonged to one-seventh of the population. This was said to be the root cause of poverty which was statistically demonstrated by Booth and by B.

S. Rowntree in his study of York.[1] Even when fully employed, large numbers of people lived in poverty because of the unevenness of wage-rates and the existence of casual labour in many industries.[2] Inadequate or irregular earnings came to be seen as a major cause of poverty.

In the last quarter of the nineteenth century there was a changing view of poverty in the minds of reformers and a growing realisation amongst the poor themselves that they could alter their conditions. This was the period of the 'New Unionism' which began to move away from the old craft unions based on skilled workers towards the organisation of unskilled workers and women workers. Although male unemployment was at the centre of the debate, the work of the women's movement ensured that the problems of women workers were also voiced. The Women's Industrial Council and similar organisations raised women's employment as a public issue and investigations such as the Select Committee on the Sweating System and the Royal Commission on Labour clearly identified women's employment as a problem. Attention was focused on the difference in wage rates between men and women and the effects of women's industrial employment on their physical and moral health and on home and family life. The general publicity given to women's employment at this time developed into a widespread concern about the effect of married women's wage work on the nation's health. Married women's work was linked to high infant mortality rates and a fear about general deterioration of the race. The linking of this physical and moral deterioration with married women's employment was influential in changing social thinking. For example, the idea of state responsibility for mothers gained credence amongst certain reformers although it was to be many years before it was actually put into practice in the form of family allowances.

The poor were coming to be seen as a threat to the social fabric and the government was faced with the problem of how to prevent them from using their new franchise to overturn a society based on capitalist wealth.[3] As it turned out, the defence against socialism was social legislation.[4] Very influential in the moves towards legislation dealing with poverty were the Fabians, in particular the Webbs. Sydney Webb 'exemplified progressive social thought of the 80s and 90s – scientific reform as opposed to deterrent poor relief'.[5] In his view, poverty was a crime because it wasted the individual and so harmed society. So, if the nation were to save itself from the threat represented by the poor, it had to introduce social reform to remove the worst aspects of poverty. The Boer War gave social reform the status of a respectable political question; the 'condition of the people' question and Imperialism became linked.[6]

Prior to the 1880s, in the sphere of economics, educated opinion closely followed the views of the economist T. H. Marshall. It was generally believed that any attempt to raise wages nationally must involve a policy of restriction on either hours or the supply of labour. According to this theory, payment must be proportional to effort. The classical emphasis on the almost perfect laws of the market remained. A minimum wage level could not be defined and high wages could only be related to improvements in efficiency, rising profit levels and changes in the relative supply of labour.[7]

By the late 1880s the policy of the minimum wage was being put forward. In *Industrial Democracy,* published in 1897, Beatrice and Sydney Webb put forward their views on the National Minimum:

> The object of the National Minimum is to secure the community against the evils of industrial parasitism, the minimum wage for a man or woman respectively would be determined by practical inquiry as to the cost of the food, clothing and shelter physiologically necessary according to the national habits and custom to prevent bodily deterioration. Such a minimum would therefore be low and through its establishment would be welcomed as a boon by the unskilled workers in the regulated industries.[8]

The Webbs maintained that the benefits for the worker would be, firstly, that the levelling up of the standard conditions of sanitation, hours and wages would stimulate demand for labour; secondly, any shrinking of the sweated industries would mean an expansion of what they called the self-supporting trades which would absorb any unemployed workers; and thirdly, new permanent jobs would be created.[9]

It was against a background of philanthropic and individual pressure, official and non-official reports and investigations that the decisive action to legislate on homework was finally taken. The Royal Commission on the Housing of the Working Classes (1884–5) did much to draw public attention to the working and living conditions of homeworkers, and in 1888 the Select Committee on the Sweating System was inaugurated. Once the Select Committee had reported back the homeworker could no longer be pushed so easily to one side, and sparked off yet further investigations and reports: a flood of articles on homeworkers followed in its wake. On 2 June 1906 the *Daily News* sponsored the famous Sweated Industries Exhibition held in the Queen's Hall, Langham Place, London. The main organisers of the exhibition were A. G. Gardiner, editor of the *Daily News*, Mary MacArthur of the Women's Trade Union League, and Margaret Macdonald of the Women's Industrial Council. Workers were seen manufacturing matchboxes, sewing various articles of clothing, carding hooks and eyes and so on. In all, forty-five trades were represented. Details of homeworkers' rates of pay and the cost of materials were given to visitors to the exhibition as well as a lecture on the sweating system. Throughout 1906 sweated industries exhibitions were organised all over the country by branches of the Anti-sweating League and the trade union movement. Newspaper reports show that sweated industries exhibitions were held in Manchester, Leicester, Birmingham, Worcester, Bristol, Cambridge, Ilford and Croydon, as well as in towns in Wales and Scotland.[10]

By the turn of the century there was widespread concern about the situation of homeworkers. Two organisations, the National Anti-sweating League and the National League to Establish a Minimum Wage took up their cause. The President of the Anti-sweating League was George Cadbury and branches were soon established in Liverpool, Manchester, Oxford, Leicester and Bristol. The wave of publicity and concern over homework reached its peak and culminated in the 1908 Select Committee on Homework.

Up to 1909 attempts at the statutory regulation of homework had been, for a variety of reasons, somewhat half-hearted. The earliest attempts at legislation in regard to homeworkers were, not surprisingly, aimed at offering protection to children. The 1860 Royal Commission on Children's Employment drew attention to the fact that large numbers of children were working in industries carried on in the home. Consequently, an Act was passed in 1864 regulating industry in residential accommodation. However, children working at home for their parents and not receiving wages were not covered by any clause in the Act. The Workshops Act of

1867 therefore extended the definition of 'employed' to mean 'occupied in any handicraft whether for wages or not, under a master or parent'. It defined a 'workshop' as 'any room or place whatever, whether in the open air or under cover, in which any handicraft is carried on by any child, young person or woman, and to which and over the young person or woman is employed has the right of access and control'. Its relevance to homeworkers still remained doubtful because the essence of homework is that it is carried on in the private dwelling of the worker, to which the employer has no right of access. It attempted to restrict the exploitation of child labour by prohibiting the employment of children under eight years of age in a home industry and those between eight and thirteen years were to be employed only as part-timers.

The 1878 Act exempted from the control of the factory inspectors private houses and rooms, but why was the government so unwilling to take decisive action in this area of the economy? The major reason seems to have been an unwillingness to extend state control into the essentially private sphere of the home. Was not an Englishman's home his castle? Mr. Henry Fawcett and many more certainly felt it their duty to speak out against a bill that proposed state intervention in this area: 'They proposed to interfere with the home of every Englishman and Englishwoman because the Bill, as it stood, would give the inspector the right to knock at his door to ascertain whether his wife and children were at work after nine o'clock at night'[11]

As well as this ideological objection to the regulation of homework there were also definite practical problems to overcome. The practical difficulties involved in administering legislation that applied to a scattered and isolated sector of the labour force are obviously great, and to these problems was added the difficulty of deciding who should be responsible for homeworkers' working conditions. Charles Booth advocated that responsibility be laid firmly on the shoulders of the landlord: the person receiving the rent should ensure that his premises were not misused by persons working illegal hours in overcrowded and insanitary conditions. On the other hand, there were those who wanted the onus of responsibility to fall upon the employer and there were others who believed that to regulate homework was to sound its death knell. The fear that regulation meant destruction of homework was a valid one in that homework survived precisely because it was exempt from the controls exercised over employment in the factories and workshops. The Select Committe on Homework stated that:

> The imposition by law of conditions and obligations upon owners and occupiers of factories and workshops tends to encourage employers to resort to Home Work in order to avoid compliance with the requirements of Parliament and the visits and supervision of the inspectors who are appointed to enforce them. The more numerous and stringent these regulations become the greater is the temptation to evade them by employing persons who work under conditions to which they do not apply.[12]

There was a certain inescapable irony in seeing legislation as the panacea for the evils of the homework system when legislation itself had given an impetus to homework.

Throughout the nineteenth century concern was expressed about women's working conditions in various areas of the economy because women and children were bracketed together as helpless beings. There was also therefore a group who agitated for reform and criticised the sweated working conditions of women because they hoped for the removal of women from the very economic sphere itself. It was considered a grave injustice that women should have to engage in wage work:

> In the case of married women, it will be generally admitted, I think, that the home should be the mother's first care. The value of maintaining a high standard in the home life of our people can hardly be averted, for upon it depends not only the present, but also the future of our race. But these poor creatures [working women] have no time to attend to the pure, tender delight of motherhood, or the many little duties which cluster around that word so sweet to the English ears – 'home'.[13]

It was pressure from a variety of quarters that created an atmosphere which was to force the hand of government, and government intervention finally came in the form of the Factory and Workshop Act of 1901. This Act was the first serious attempt to legislate on homework. Under the 1901 Act employers were required to keep lists of the names and addresses of all homeworkers in their employment. These lists had to be forwarded twice yearly to the local authority. The factory inspector could demand from the employer a list of his homeworkers and visit their homes. However, he had no authority to act to improve the conditions he might find. The usefulness of the list varied from one region to another according to the vigilance of the local authority. These lists were used by the 1907 West Ham Enquiry and were found to be very unsatisfactory. They found them inaccurate and out of date.[14] This was hardly surprising, given the nature of homework. The lists were based on a census taken on only two days in the year and would therefore not cover all homeworkers as all trades provided essentially irregular or seasonal employment. In certain areas the sending in of lists coincided with a slack period in a trade and were therefore particularly inaccurate, also homeworkers would sometimes appear on more than one list because they worked for more than one employer. Lastly, the lists only covered the homeworkers who took the work out and not the other women and children who assisted them or to whom they subcontracted work.

Under the 1901 Act employers of homeworkers were also obliged to supply their employees with written particulars of their terms of employment. Before the work was done, the employer had to supply the homeworker with the details of the work to be done and the price to be paid for it. The West Ham Inquiry found that this requirement was often not carried out by employers. The employment of persons working in insanitary conditions was forbidden under this Act. Homework was prohibited in places where there was infectious disease such as scarlet fever or smallpox.

The 1901 Act seems to have been fairly ineffective. One problem was the shortage of factory inspectors. The first women factory inspectors had been appointed in 1893 but numbers were not large enough to make the Act effective. In 1906 the annual statistics published by the Home Office revealed that 1201 cases of outwork in insanitary premises had been detected, but in only three cases out of 816 notices served were there prosecutions for non-compliance with the notice of the local authority.[15] Sanitary inspectors were criticised for not being rigorous enough and they in turn were critical of the Act, which many felt did not go far enough.[16]

The 1901 Act came up against the difficulty, which has never been successfully overcome, of attempting to regulate what in many ways is an invisible sector of the economy. The period between the turn of the century and the 1909 Trade Boards Act was one in which various private member's bills were drafted. Tennant and Dilke's bill of 1899 aimed at placing the responsibility for the conditions under which work was done on the giver-out of work and administration in the hands of the local authority. One obvious problem here was the difficulty of tracing the giver-out of work when subcontracting was so common. In 1906 the Women's Industrial Council drafted their Bill for the Better Regulation of Homework:

> The object of the Bill is to protect the public against the dissemination of disease and dirt by wearing apparel, and other articles, made in insanitary dwelling places, and to protect the workers themselves against unhealthy and vicious conditions over which they can exercise no control. The Bill introduces no new standards of sanitation, and imposes no conditions beyond those already recognised by the Factories and Workshops and the Public Health Acts. It has been drafted to correct many admitted failures in the administration of these Acts.[17]

The Women's Industrial Council's bill proposed that a factory inspector visit the premises in which the work was to be carried out and grant a certificate if it was considered suitable. The premises were to be inspected every six months and the certificate withdrawn if the conditions deteriorated. Employers giving out work to uncertified places should, they argued, be prosecuted.

The debate about the regulation of homework continued. In 1903 the Employment of Children Act gave increased statutory protection to children employed in any labour, but as always with homework, evasion was not difficult. Finally, the emphasis of the homework debate shifted from working conditions to wages. The next important piece of legislation was not an attempt to improve upon the main tenets of the Factory and Workshop Act of 1901 but an attempt to ensure the payment of legal minimum rates. B. H. Hutchins, amongst others, argued that a minimum rate was a necessity for homework.[18] However, there were many difficulties in the way of establishing minimum rates and the minimum rate could be avoided in particular home industries without too much difficulty. For example, in an industry such as chain-making, employers could arrange to sell the iron and buy the chain instead of paying wages. Another example is tailoring which provided a variety of obstacles in the way of establishing minimum rates. It was a trade in which it was difficult to draw a demarcation line between employer and employee because many homeworkers also subcontracted, albeit, on a small scale. Who was responsible for payment of a minimum rate? In tailoring, with a variety of classes of work, the establishment of a minimum rate could in some instances serve to sanction payment of a very low rate for certain types of worker. For example, some machinists could earn above the suggested minimum hourly rate of 3½d. per hour. A statutory minimum rate also failed to take into account the fact that different classes of worker incurred different expenses, which had a decisive effect on earning potential.

The instrument to ensure payment of a statutory minimum rate was a trade board. A trade board involved the transference of decisions about wage rates from the whims of the individual employer to a more representative collectivity. At the time of its introduction the Trade Boards Act was considered a radical piece of legislation. The boards were to consist of members representing employers and members representing workers in equal proportions, and of official members. District Trade Committees could be set up under the Act consisting partly of members of the trade board and partly of persons not of the trade board.[19]

The Act specifically stated that women were eligible for membership and it was required that at least one woman should be an appointed member of every board for a trade in which women were largely employed and that homeworkers should be represented on the boards of trade in which a considerable proportion of homeworkers were engaged.[20]

Decisions of the trade board were enforced by inspectors. Employers who failed to pay the minimum rates could be forced to make up the arrears and were liable to a maximum fine of £20. They could also be fined forty shillings for failing to display in a prominent position in the factory or warehouse the details of wage rates to be paid for each work order. However, homeworkers were seldom confident enough and often too ignorant of their legal rights to challenge an employer or inform an inspector.

The first Trade Boards Act of 1909 was directed at the least skilled and weakest workers. The four home industries covered by the Act were ready-made wholesale tailoring, cardboard-box-making, chain-making and machine-made lace and net finishing.

The minimum time rates fixed were 3¼d. per hour in tailoring, 2½d. per hour in chainmaking, 3d. in boxmaking and 2¾d. in lacemaking. Only one rate was fixed for each trade irrespective of the variety of processes involved.

R. H. Tawney has estimated that the total number of women homeworkers employed in those sections of the tailoring industry affected by the trade board was between fifteen and twenty-two thousand.[21] In 1909, finishing was still the most important component of homework in tailoring, being the process demanding least skill. Prior to the 1909 Act wages in tailoring were at their lowest in the areas of the country in which homework predominated – that is, in London and the eastern counties. The Tailoring Trade Board set only minimum-time rates and left it to the employer to fix piece-rates. Thus the system was open to abuses and Tawney's investigations revealed that by 1914 only a very small number of homeworkers' rates had been advantageously affected by the legislation. Out of a total of ninety-five homeworkers in the Colchester district he found less than half were earning the minimum time rate. Out of four hundred and twenty-five homeworkers in East London only about half were earning the minimum time rate.[22]

The Chainmaking Trade Board affected the earnings of about two thousand female homeworkers. Delay over payment of the new legal minimum rates led to an almost unprecedented action amongst homeworkers, that is, the strike of 1910.

The Anti-sweating League had argued for trade boards in the hope that they would put an end to low paid labour.[23] Both Gertrude Tuckwell and Mary MacArthur advocated the setting up of wages boards to regulate wages in low paying industries employing large numbers of women, both in factories and as homeworkers. As well as raising the rate of wages, Mary MacArthur suggested that it would be a very valuable weapon in organising the workers in these industries: 'If we raised their wages even a little we would be able to organise them and so improve the general conditions.'[24] Miss Clara Collet, Senior Investigator for the Women's Industries to the Board of Trade, was also in favour of wages boards. Indeed, the women's trade union movement must take much of the credit for the campaign against sweating that finally forced the government's hand in the field of legislation.

There is little doubt that the trade boards improved earnings for many of the most sweated homeworkers. However. they were inadequate in that they provided no guidance on determining the minimum rates which meant a diverse rather than a consistent and uniform criteria of assessment. The 1913 Act brought four other trades under the control of trade boards – shirt-making, confectionery, hollow-ware and tin-box-making and by 1921 there were thirty-five trade boards in existence.

The Trade Boards Act was the last piece of legislation to make any real impact on homework. Trade boards were succeeded by wages councils in 1945,[25] yet homework has continued to fall outside the scope of most legislation. The boards did improve wages for many homeworkers but in so doing they deprived the employer of a major incentive for employing them. Thus legislation may well have contributed to a decline in the availability of homework. However, the many loopholes in the limited amount of legislation directed at homework and the insurmountable difficulties of administering the legislation left the majority of employers plenty of room for manoeuvre. It must also be remembered that the homeworkers themselves collaborated in the evasion of the Acts. Most homeworkers were desperate for work and generally ignorant of their rights and hence accepted work on terms dictated wholly by the employer. Employers, aided by subcontracting, did not go out of their way to publicise their homework sector and the women themselves were often eager to keep their work a secret. This conspiracy of silence has always worked against the successful adminstration of legislation.

The debate on legislation and the question of homework and unionisation are closely linked. There has always been confusion and discussion about which is likely to solve the problem of homeworking. Why did homeworkers fail to organise themselves into trade unions or to join already established unions or societies in attempt to better their working conditions and rates of pay? Unionisation of working women was slow to get off the ground. There were several major problems inherent in any attempts to organise women workers in the late nineteenth and early twentieth centuries. Some related to the women themselves and some to the attitude of male workers towards them. There were six problem areas. First, the character of women's occupations. Women were generally employed as semi-skilled or unskilled workers amongst whom trade unionism was late to develop. Thus, the problem of women in trade unions does not only refer to their sex but forms part of the larger problem of organising semi-skilled or unskilled workers. Because there was no scarcity of unskilled workers, they had little bargaining power with the employers. Unlike unions of skilled workers, their unions would be relatively powerless in an industrial dispute, so it would be comparatively easy for employers to bring in blackleg labour. This militated against unskilled workers forming or joining trade unions.[26]

The second problem relates to the low wages earned by most women workers. They were difficult to organise because they were badly paid, and badly paid because they were difficult to organise.[27] Low wages meant that it was often not possible for them to pay trade union subscriptions. A third major barrier to organisation of women workers was the attitude of male trade unionist. Many men regarded women as necessarily unskilled, almost casual, labour and believed them to be a menace to their own precarious standard of living. In spite of male opposition, in all the new light engineering industries and clerical occupations, women were being taken on at cheaper rates of pay; sometimes at less than half the rate that men could command. The response of male workers was not to include women in their own jealously guarded craft organisations but to oppose their employment as much as they could. Attempts were made to drive them down to as small a number of trades and as small a number of work processes within those trades as possible.[28] But the old-time trade unionists' argument against the admission of women was not based wholly on economic grounds. It was a 'mixture of economics and sentiment'.[29] The policy of the barred door for women was consistent with the prevailing domestic ideology. Even those unions which gave the most attention and access to women as participants, especially certain cotton unions, the type of participation and the nature of their involvement was not generally the same as that of the man in the industry.[30] It was assumed that women's work was marginal in terms of their lives. It was also felt to be marginal to the area of work which was concerned in terms of men's labour.[31] Another hurdle in the way of organising women was antagonism on the part of employers, who saw any attempts to persuade women to join trade unions as an attack on their cheap and docile labour force.[32]

The two final problems relate to the interrupted way in which women worked throughout their lives and their attitudes to their work. The way in which women viewed their time spent in paid work outside the home as temporary and the way married women often viewed their work as peripheral meant that they were less likely to combine for better wages and working conditions. Nevertheless, in spite of these not inconsiderable obstacles to the organisation of women workers, individual women and women in the Women's Industrial Council persevered in their attempts to better the lot of women workers.

Emma Paterson formed the Women's Protective and Provident League in 1873 with the aim of establishing unions in every trade in which women worked. The climate of opinion among male union leaders towards women workers was characterised by opposition and hostility. Henry Broadhurst, a prominent trade union leader, declared to the 1877 TUC:

> It was their duty as men and husbands to use their utmost efforts to bring about a condition of things where their wives should be in their proper sphere at home, seeing after the house and family instead of being dragged into competition against the great and strong men of the world.[33]

The Women's Protective and Provident League avoided the word 'union' in its title to appease the wealthy supporters on which it initially depended. It provided the major impetus for the unionisation of women workers.

In 1876 Emma Paterson became first woman delegate to the TUC, where she opposed Protective Legislation laws controlling the working conditions of women and children. By classing women with children, they suggested that women were unable to protect themselves. Since women were not represented in Parliament, she felt that men had no right to pass legislation which affected them. From 1889 the League dropped some of its philanthropic schemes and concentrated on industrial work.[34] It became the Women's Trade Union League, and in 1888 Clementina Black, who replaced Emma Paterson, successfully moved the first Equal Pay Resolution at the TUC. From this date, the League offered the services of a woman organiser to any union with women members affiliated. The organisers were paid eighteen shillings a week and travelled all over the country. The were nearly all working-class women with personal experience of industrial conditions. The League played an essential role in the successful strike of the match-girls in 1888. It helped to spread trade unionism to groups previously outside its sphere of influence, such as clerks and shop assistants, during the 1890s. In all, about eighty to ninety societies were established by the League, although many were of an ephemeral nature.

Women's trade unionism was assisted by the wave of 'new unionism' in the 1880s. In the early 1890s Lady Dilke of the Women's Trade Union League said of the 'new unionism':

What is called the 'new unionism' which first attracted notice during the struggle at the docks appears, on examination, to be but the old unionism proceeding by more hazardous and sensational methods, yet it has done good service to the cause, and especially to the cause which the Women's Trade Union League has in hand, in two ways. In the first place, by appealing to the element of sentiment which always plays a large part in the decisions of the British public, the 'new unionism' has struck a great blow at the root of the prejudice which has long lingered against combination for any but 'friendly' purposes, and in the second, it has shown that it is possible to organise with effect – if only for a time – the least skilled and most underpaid forms of labour; that is to say, it has touched the very classes amongst which the league is most desirous of promoting combination.[35]

In 1906 the new secretary of the WTUL, Mary MacArthur, amalgamated most of the small unions founded by the league into a general labour union – the National Federation of Women Workers – and became its first General Secretary. The *Woman Worker* was launched – a penny weekly with a peak circulation of 20 000. Membership of the NFWW grew from 2000 at the end of its first year to 20 000 in 1914. The Federation was especially concerned with the country's poorest paid female workers. It was the driving force in the pre-First World War campaign to end the sweating of the homework labour force. Throughout the First World War it remained active as it fought to protect the rights of many new groups of women workers. In 1921 it amalgamated with the National Union of General and Municipal Workers. The Women's Trade Union

League had ceased to exist as an independent body the previous year and had become the women's department of the Trades Union Council. After the First World War there were 1 086 000 women trade unionists in 383 trade unions. Of these, 36 were exclusive female unions.[36] The war pushed up women's membership of trade unions by 60 per cent although unfortunately it was to slump with the end of the war.

As regards the difficulties of organising homeworkers into trade unions, Gertrude Tuckwell, Chairwoman of the Women's Trade Union League, said in response to the question of the Chairman of the Select Committee on Homework about the organisation of homeworkers:

> Yes it is absolutely impossible . . . an attempt was [also] made to organise women homeworkers in the tailoring trade and nothing could be done and the organisation went to pieces. So when I became more actively connected with the League we had inquiries made to see what could be done in the way of trying to put in force any legislation that existed and getting further legislation because we could not do anything in the way of organisation with these homeworkers . . .[37]

Another member of the Committee, Mr Arthur Dewar, asked Gertrude Tuckwell whether she had persevered for a long time to organise the tailoring outworkers' trade. This was her response:

> I think so, we always persevere for a long time . . . I think all the usual steps were tried. But you cannot organise these workers because to organise people you must have people who are not so much depressed by working night and day that they have no time to think. You must have people who have some sort of power of acting corporately who are not entirely scattered.[38]

Gertrude Tuckwell's principal argument in her evidence was that the problem of low wages was the central one to be solved in the case of homeworkers and that if the rate of wages were raised the other problems of working conditions and so on would also be solved.[39]

The homeworker was unlikely to feel confident enough to attempt to better her work situation and terms of employment since her employment was so insecure. So homeworkers, the people most in need of organisation, were those least likely and least able to organise themselves. A Study of women's work in 1894 concluded that:

> Where work is done wholly at home, it is difficult to bring direct influence to bear upon the women to induce them to combine, and yet it is here that combination is most necessary since the workers have neither the support of companionship nor the protection of the Factory Acts.[40]

The biggest problem in the way of unionising homeworkers has always been the isolation these women experience. Indeed, there must have been relatively few homeworkers who had even heard ideas about unionisation being discussed. Homeworkers have always formed an essentially privatised sector of the labour force. Clementina Black of the Women's Industrial Council was forced to conclude that:

> Homeworkers, are, of course, especially isolated, and the successful organisation of a union among female homeworkers would be an industrial miracle not looked for by the most sanguine toiler in the industrial field.[41]

Scattered and isolated from one another and cut off from the factory labour force, there was little opportunity for feelings of solidarity and comradeship to develop. Indeed, the homeworker could be a positive hindrance to the spread of female trade unionism. In 1890 the Select Committee on the Sweating System stated:

> With respect to the low wages and excessive hours of labour, we think that good may be effected by the extension of co-operative societies and by well-considered co-operation among the workers. We are aware that homeworkers form a great obstacle in the way of combination, inasmuch as they cannot be readily brought to combine for the purpose of raising wages. To remove this obstacle we have been urged to recommend the prohibition by legislation of working at home, but we think such a measure would be arbitrary and oppressive, not sanctioned by any

precedent in existing law, and impossible to be effectually enforced.[42]

The bargaining position of the indoor worker was weakened by the very existence of homeworkers. Employers could always threaten to give work out to homeworkers if indoor labourers decided to take industrial action or refused to accept reductions in rates of pay. Clara Collett claimed that the 'facility and readiness with which City firms take advantage of this hindrance to communication between workers is unequalled by anything in the East End'.[43] Women homeworkers were said to have been used as strike breakers and to lower the level of wages.

The composition of the homework labour force differed from the indoor hands in that the majority of the former were essentially casual or seasonal workers. Homework was also commonly of an inferior quality to that done in the factory. This made it more difficult to argue that homeworkers should be paid the same as indoor hands. Of course, a number of homeworkers did join the same union to which the indoor workers of their particular trade belonged, but these were in the minority.

The situation was yet further complicated by the fact that it was not always possible to draw a clear line of demarcation between factory hand and homeworker. Large numbers of female factory workers received little more pay than homeworkers and were therefore forced to supplement their earnings. In 1908, Mary MacArthur's paper, *The Woman Worker,* reported:

> After a hard day in the factory they toil into the small hours making garments, cardboard boxes, or artificial flowers, or carding hooks and eyes. An instance was lately brought to light of a number of girls who made under-clothing being asked by their employer, in defiance of the Factory Acts, to take work home and finish it. They were in the habit of working until two in the morning. What else was possible? Their wage (factory and homework included) amounted to just over 7s. a week.

The homeworker's attitude to her work was a further obstacle in the way of her developing a trade union consciousness. Given that most homework was dull, monotonous, unskilled and sweated labour it is not surprising that these women did not see work as a major area of interest. Clementina Black, in her pre-First World War survey of married women's work, found that:

> Women working at the sweated industries such as brush-drawing, box making, blousemaking, etc. take little interest or pride in their work, find it exceedingly irksome and arduous and thankfully relinquish it on marriage if possible. When asked why they are working the answer is almost invariably that, for one reason or another, the family cannot get on without it. The few who can command a high wage at skilled work such as fur-stitchers, gold embroiderers and the more expert mantle-makers seem to view it from an entirely different point of view.

The hostility of male workers to homework was yet another problem. A majority of male trade unionists wished to abolish homework which was seen as a threat to the strength of the bargaining position of indoor labour. Many believed that organising homework labour would consolidate its position and perpetuate its existence as an economic system. In its campaign to unionise homeworkers the women's trade union movement received at best only spasmodic and localised support from male trade unionists and at worst, active hostility.

The women's trade union movement of the 1880s vigorously attacked the problem of sweated homework labour. However, in the following twenty years the leaders of the movement were forced to shift from a position that saw mass unionisation as the panacea for the abuses arising from the homework system to one that advocated state intervention and statutory regulation of wages and working conditions of homeworkers. During the 1880s the Women's Trade Union League met with a number of limited successes in their campaign to organise homeworkers, but they were generally only short-lived. The 1890 Annual Report of the Women's Protective and Provident League provides us with an account of a meeting at which the League attempted to unionise matchbox-makers. The report is particularly interesting in that it shows clearly the factors which combined to force the women's trade union movement to alter the emphasis of their campaign. The meeting was convened on 23 November 1889 in the Holy Trinity Church of Shoreditch. Shoreditch and Bethnal Green possessed a heavy concentration of matchbox-makers and the inaugural meeting was well attended:

The women took a very intelligent interest in the suggestions made to them from the platform with regard to improving their condition . . . and a business meeting was arranged the following week. To this, few came, and the difficulty of finding amongst the workers themselves any woman with sufficient time to devote to working up the union, necessitated the abandonment of the effort till other help could be obtained. On May 18th, a tea was given to which all women working in the matchbox trade were invited. Over three hundred came and during tea Lady Dilke and Miss Routledge talked to the women about the chances of forming a society. The difficulty to be contended against in organising the matchbox-makers, does not consist in inability on their part to grasp the principles of unionism. The husbands of many of them are members of the Dock Labourers Union, and they listen with intelligent interest to a discussion of the question of combination. They all, however, work in their own homes, their labour is unskilled labour, and their children help with the easier portions of the work. The fact that matchbox making is not carried on in factories, makes it specifically difficult to induce the women to attempt combination.[46]

Experiences such as this led the Women's Trade Union League to conclude that unionisation could not provide the whole answer. In 1907 Miss Gertrude Tuckwell, President of the Women's Trade Union League, commented 'that her experience had brought prominently to her notice the impossibility of combination among homeworkers . . . The truth was that such people were unable to help themselves'.[47] A year later, in 1908, Mary MacArthur's trade union paper, *The Woman Worker,* drew the following pessimistic conclusions about homework:

Trade unionism is helpless here. So long as it is unable to control or restrict the supply of labour, trade unionism can do nothing. And the sweated workers are too isolated and browbeaten to combine. We must look still to the public conscience, expressing itself through just legislation.

The first step is a minimum wage, legally enforced. No other remedy will serve.[48]

From 1890 the WTUL advocated a policy of state intervention

and government regulation. Homework remained one of the burning issues of the women's trade union movement up to the Trade Boards Act of 1909. It is an impossible task to produce any meaningful statistics concerning homework and union membership. Numbers were seldom mentioned and the turnover of the labour force and the often short-lived success of homework unions served to make statistics almost immediately out of date.

The National Anti-sweating League (NASL), formed in 1906, was established with the intention of organising women's labour and awakening public opinion and interest in female labour. It was particularly concerned with homework. It campaigned for the establishment of trade boards, and sought to provide alternative employment for workers sacked from their own jobs as a result of trying to better their working conditions through joining or forming a trade union. The Homeworkers' League was set up under the auspices of the NASL with the object of protecting the interests of homeworkers and providing a means of social contact and association between workers. They opened a Homeworkers' Hall at their headquarters in Bethnal Green.[49] Membership was open to homeworkers in all trades and the subscription was one penny a month. Homeworkers could take their complaints to the League which would in turn take them up with the official authorities. In the 1908 Select Committee on Homework Miss Vynne refers to the Homeworkers' League as possessing a membership of about three thousand.[50] The Homeworkers' League was, however, opposed to wages boards, although it was not against government intervention *per se*.

By the early part of this century many campaigners against sweating had recognised that the solution did not lie with unionisation or statutory legislation but with a combination of the two. Sydney Webb was one of those who reached such a conclusion:

> Where, as is usually the case, female labour is employed for practically unskilled work, needing only the briefest experience; or where the work, though skilled, is of a kind into which every woman is initiated as part of her general education, no combination will ever be able to enforce, by its own power, any Standard Rate, any Normal Day, or any definite conditions of sanitation and safety.[51]

However, for many, the passing of the Trade Boards Act was seen as the successful conclusion to the problem. For example, in the *Women's Trade Union Review* of 1913, J. J. Mallon stated that:

> The substance of the matter is that the legal minimum wage, so far from being an alternative to vigorous trade unionism, will serve as an incentive and prop to combination.
>
> Never in England has it been possible to organise large bodies of homeworkers, but since the passing of the Trade Boards Act this miracle has been accomplished in at least two districts – in Cradley Heath where every man and woman outworker in the chain trade is now a member of a Trade Union, and in Nottingham, where some thousands of women are in the process of being enrolled.[52]

The Trade Boards were obviously seen as providing the impetus for this successful unionisation, as Mallon goes on to say:

> In both these trades the organised men have spent from time to time sums of money amounting to thousands of pounds in abortive attempts to organise the outworkers. An impossible job they said at last, and dropped it. The impossible job has since been accomplished – to the surprise of all beholders, and notably to that of the general secretaries of these men's unions, who as late as 1909 were entirely pessimistic as to any prospect of organisation.[53]

However, this presented too rosy a picture of the situation and even Mallon was forced to add a cautionary, less optimistic paragraph pointing out that this success did not spill over into '. . . the poor districts of great towns where homeworkers are still plentiful. In particular, they do not touch the East of London.'[54]

A strike is a rare event in a chronicle of the history of homework labour: a successful one even rarer. Thus the Cradley Heath strike has a special place in the history of women's labour.

The lot of the female chainmaker was an exceptionally hard one. A minority of women worked in the chain factory but the majority worked in forges in their own back yards. Most of the work was 'country work' such as chains for farm horses and carts. Despite its manual nature, women often started working in the trade at an early age. One woman, taught by her mother, had started making chains at eleven years of age. In 1905 she was earning 2s. 6d. a week working Monday to Friday from 7.00 am to 7.00 pm and until 2 o'clock on Saturdays.[55] The work was physically very demanding, whether the women were struggling up the Cradley Hill with bundles of iron on their shoulders or whether they were working in the forge, blistering and disfiguring their hands. Inevitably the infant mortality rate was high: within a few days of the birth the woman returned with her baby to continue her work in the forge. In 1910 the *Daily News* estimated that there were about 1300 women employed in chain-making.

Chain-making was the first trade in which the minimum wage was enforced. The trade board proposal was a minimum wage of 2½d. per hour for the hammered section of the trade. On May 17th 1910 notice was given of the proposed rates. During the following three months objections were heard and on 17th August final notice was given. From that time the chain-makers were entitled to the new rates unless they had signed an agreement to the contrary. A 'petition' drawn up by the employers delayed the payment of these rates by a further six months. Many of the chain-makers, unable to read or write, innocently made their mark on the employers' 'petition'. The employers saw this six months as a time in which they could stockpile work. Thus a long period of slackness would have followed the introduction of the legal rates. Those refusing to sign to accept the lower rates were locked out and there was a great deal of anger amongst those women who had been tricked into signing. In the September of 1910 about eight hundred women were locked out. About three hundred and fifty women were members of the National Federation of Women Workers (NFWW) and entitled to five shillings per week 'lock out' pay. The Women's Trade Union League guaranteed that all women locked out should receive a minimum sum of four shillings a week.[56] The support of the women's Trade Union Movement was essential to the successful outcome of the strike. Morale seems to have been high amongst the strikers, aided by the continuing support of the NFWW. The high morale of the strikers is expressed through the words of Mrs Patience Round, who by the time of the strike had been working sixty-nine years as a chain-maker:

These are wonderful times. I never thought I should live to assert the rights of us women. It has been the week of my life – three meetings and such beautiful talking . . . In the whole of my life I have never stopped working in the shop for more than two days.[57]

The NFWW seems to have been able to harness a feeling of solidarity and comradeship. Respect from the chain-makers for the work of the Union is expressed in their songs, of which the following, sung to the tune of 'John Brown's Body', is an example.[58]

Strike! Strike! Strike! a blow for Freedom every time,
Cast your chains away from you upon the ground;
Strike! Strike! Strike! a blow for Freedom every time,
As you go marching round.

Now come along and join the Union,
Don't let us have to ask you twice –
Now come along and joing the Union,
All fighting for our price.

Another, sung to the tune of 'Yankee Doodle'.

The Chain Masters came along,
With their fine agreement:
They asked us all to sign our names,
For taking lower payment.

Then the Union came alone,
Said – do you want your price, oh!
We said – we do – they didn't have
To ask the question twice, oh!

Mary MacArthur in particular was held in great respect and affection by the chain-makers. The strike received a large amount of publicity through the press and both local and national coverage seems to have been sympathetic to the women. Favourable publicity meant a good response to the strike fund, which reached £4000. One woman recalled how twelve of the chain-makers had gone to London to collect for the strike. However, the police, supposedly mistaking them for suffragists, had arrested them and kept them in prison overnight.[59] Presumably other attempts at fund raising did not end so badly.

Good organisation of the strikers by the NFWW backed up by the WTUL and the NASL can take much of the credit for the success of the strike. However, there was also another important contributory factor that made the thirteen-week strike a victory for the chain-makers. Chain-makers, unlike the majority of homeworkers, were concentrated within a specific locality. Chain-making was also work that demanded a particular type of skill and equipment and one presumes that there were not a large number of women available to take their places.

In 1913, just prior to the great upheaval of the First World War, the second Trade Boards Act was passed and the success of the Cradley Heath strike was still fresh in people's minds. However, Cradley Heath was to prove to be something of a unique event rather than a pattern of industrial action that homeworkers were going to emulate in the future. The war was just around the corner and, not surprisingly, homework ceased to be a major focus of interest and concern for the trade union movement at that time.

8

Homework, 1945–1985

In the years immediately preceding the First World War and during the early stages of the war itself, women's unemployment was severe. A number of traditional women's trades such as dressmaking and millinery were in the throes of a depression. During the period from the first Trade Boards Act up to 1914 a few sporadic attempts were made to alleviate the situation. For example, the Central Unemployed Body for London opened up a number of sewing rooms in which unemployed women made garments for sale in the marketplace. Various philanthropic ventures were made along the same lines by concerned individuals but these failed to make any real impact on the situation. Indeed, many of the well-intentioned acts of philanthropy merely took work from one sector of women and gave it to another.

A more serious attempt to deal with the problem of female unemployment came in the early stages of the war with the establishment of the Central Committee on Women's Employment. This committee did at least acknowledge that female unemployment was a real problem and that it had to be tackled seriously and not in the former haphazard manner. The secretary of the committee, Mary MacArthur, slanted the aims of the organisation in the direction of education, technical training and provision of tuition for women in specific trades. Its main aim was to devise schemes of employment for women. However, it was open only to those who formerly had been in employment. This policy no doubt excluded many women who had done homework and hence been employed only on a casual basis. The minimum rate of pay was

126

3d. an hour with a maximum working week of forty hours.[1] However, in attempting to put into practice the above aims the committee and other similar organisations were fighting against a tide of public opinion that gave no recognition to the benefits and importance of training a potential female labour force. It was the progress of the war itself that was to provide the tremendous stimulus required to result in a complete upheaval and tumult of accepted ideas about women's role in the economy that would finally result in recognition being given to the value of female labour.

As the war progressed women and girls were positively encouraged to leave the home and go into industry, and under the flag of patriotism many women were overworked and underpaid. The imposition of universal conscription was the decisive factor and in November 1915 the Home Secretary and President of the Board of Trade established the Women's Employment Committee. Women left their traditional jobs and flocked into 'men's jobs' in order to meet the demands of a war economy.

During the war the number of women employed in industry increased by over one million, with approximately 700 000 directly replacing men.[2] Whereas in July 1914, 212 000 women were employed in the metal and engineering industries, by July 1917 the figures had reached 819 000. The largest proportionate increase in women's employment during the war was, in fact, in transport, with 18 000 employed in 1914 and 117 000 by 1918.[3] The peak of the demand for female labour was from January 1916 to July 1918. The 1911 Census showed a total of nearly 6 000 000 women employed: about 1.75 million of these were in domestic service. The Board of Trade estimate was that by 1916, 100 000 had left domestic service.[4] Women were also recruited from the ranks of homeworkers, many continued in work after marriage and married women and widows returned to employment, girls were recruited straight from school and many middle-class women entered the labour market for the first time. The net increase in female workers employed outside the home comparing July 1914 with the end of the war, was about 1 200 000 – an increase of 500 000 in industry and 352 000 in business.[5]

The Home Office permitted the relaxation of the Factory Acts. Shift work, long hours, Sunday work and shorter mealtimes all became the norm, as did working conditions which constituted a definite danger to health. The trade union movement assisted the government by also relaxing their vigilance.

Recruitment of women into the war industries was an easy task. To many it meant for the first time a much needed and regular income. Wages were higher than their previous earnings. Numbers of women were also only too happy to leave traditional types of 'women's work' – in particular, domestic service. patriotism was a further incentive. In fact, patriotism displaced the former dominant ideology of feminine domesticity as the major ideological force governing women's choice of employment. Everything from taking women out of their own homes and away from their families to low pay and long hours was justified in the name of patriotism. For example, work in munitions was particularly demanding and dangerous work. Hours were very long while the threat of explosions and exposure to chemicals were ever-present hazards. Lilian Barker, while holding the post of Lady Superintendent at Woolwich Arsenal, drafted notices in the following forceful vein:

> Motive for work: Patriotism. A munition worker is as important as the soldier in the trenches, and on her his life depends.

> Aim: Output. Anyone who limits this is a traitor to sweethearts, husbands and brothers fighting. One minute lost by sixty girls means the loss of one hour's output. This includes slacking at meals and at closing time.

> Happiness: If any worker does not like her job, she should give it up; she will be of no use, and probably a bad influence.[6]

The notice demands obedience to the dictates of the superintendent. Implicit in the wording is the fact that a patriotic woman does not think of raising questions about her hours of work or her working conditions. By definition a patriotic woman enjoys hard work. The ideology of patriotism helped to foster an acquiescent attitude and guarded against any likely militancy in the new female labour force.

There was, of course, another side to this picture. Patriotism and a war economy could work in the women's favour. They produced forces that were instrumental in breaking down many of the former prejudices relating to women and their employment. A majority of women obviously enjoyed their new-found, if only temporary, 'freedom'. Above all, many women welcomed the companionship of other women to which their work introduced them. A feeling of community and comradeship often developed out of these new work relationships. These sentiments are expressed through the words of one woman who had worked at making shells in a Liverpool munitions factory:

> I started there in July 1915 – there 'til 1917 – 'til I was having me second baby. I stayed until I was nearly four weeks off me time. Oh, the girls was lovely. You know, we all knew one another and they were all married women – we all understood – oh, and they all went mad when I said, – I'll have to be leaving soon and when I told 'em why – ooh, oh, Katy, why didn't you watch out. Well, I said I couldn't help these things. You know we were all like – ah, awful happy.[7]

This comradeship and the feeling of being part of things was a positive feature of the war work but the work itself was often very strenuous. For example, in the Colchester tailoring factories, women worked on government contracts making military uniforms. Women working in the factories in Colchester remembered the heavy and hard nature of the work:

> *When you did the uniforms was that very hard work? It was heavy wasn't it, the khaki?*
> Well, you would do it in parts, you see, but the one what put the sleeves in and finished it off that was the heaviest part, the last one. I used to what they call 'bag 'em off', that was heavy work but in the summer we used to do the overcoats and in the winter we used to do the shirts. Well that was hot and hard work.

The factory made some economies during the war:

> During the war, we all had a cardboard box and we used to have to put it at the back, you know, the arm of the machine. We used to stand the box just at the back and every piece of cotton that you cut off for every seam you had to put it in that box and they sent that back to the firm and had it all spun up again.

The Colchester factories also made palliasses for the army:

I didn't make the clothes for the soldiers. I used to sort of fit them. Used to do the coats you see. They had no linings, khaki. I used to have to fit them all ready . . . this was the First World War this . . . 1916, I think, we had a contract to make the palliasses for the soldiers' beds. You know, six foot long they were and a sort of unbleached calico and when they left our factory they had to be stuffed with straw . . . we used to have to get so many out a day, must've done thousands. I was in charge of them you see and I rushed them through. Of course, you thought you were doing something for the war like that you see and also used to make the tunics. Khaki tunics. We earned vey little money, about seven shillings a week, in those days.

Many of the informants spoke of the long hours, low wages and arduous work in the tailoring factories in war-time. They felt, however, that they were contributing to the war effort in the best way they could, by making uniforms and palliasses for soldiers at the front.

The link between the women working on the home front making uniforms and the soldiers fighting abroad is nicely brought out in the following quote from a woman who started work in one of the Colchester tailoring factories at the age of thirteen in 1916:

During the First World War did you make uniforms at Hart and Levy?
Oh yes, that was the main thing when I went to Hart and Levy's at 13. They were all on khaki uniforms you see. We used to fell what they call the bandage pocket, that's a little pocket just inside here, oblong pocket and we used to fell them right round and close them right up and all the girls used to put notes in them and several of them had letters come back.
Oh, did they?
Yes. Because they didn't open them up until the man that was going to have the coat . . . then I suppose he opened them to put the bandages in then he read these notes that the girls had put in. Oh, there was a lot of that and they used to get letters back.
I wonder if there were any romances!
Oh, I daresay there was, of course, I was too young, but I knew they used to do it because I used to fell them round like . . . They were hard because they were stiff. You know how a man do up a

military coat with two bigs hooks and eyes here and you have to
fell these hooks and they had to be strong. They were hard to
work on.

War work brought to many women a regular wage, a relative
independence and companionship. It was particularly attractive
when seen in relation to the pre-war major employer of female
labour, domestic service. The Women's Advisory Committee
Report of 1919 concluded after its investigation into the 'domestic
service problem', that lack of social status, long hours of duty and
absence of companionship were the chief causes of the shortage in
supply of domestic servants that developed at this time.[8]

At the time of the outbreak of the First World War women's
average industrial wage was 11s. 7d. – that is, one third the average
male industrial wage, but for the majority of women engaged in paid
employment earnings were a great deal lower than that. In 1911,
domestic servants formed 36 per cent of female wage earners. In
occupations such as domestic service, dressmaking, millinery and
shop work up to the First World War women were receiving a
significant proportion of their wages in the form of board and
lodging with only a small cash payment in addition. Even larger
numbers of women working as wives and mothers had been
receiving no cash payment at all. For a majority of women the war
drastically altered this situation and women received wages in the
form of a cash payment, as they were absorbed into the war
economy. Women had to decide how their earnings should be spent
and thus achieved a greater independence. The 'living-in' system
experienced a significant decline as a result of the war and it was
never again to recover its pre-war predominance.

The large demand for female labour during the four years of a war
economy introduced significant numbers of women into a variety of
employments that had previously been closed to them. A side effect
of allowing women access to employment that did not involve
traditional female work roles was that women experienced a new
relationship to their economic role. The different forms of
employment women that engaged in during the war, or the very fact
that they took up employment for the first time, or in the case of
married women, returned to paid employment, encouraged a
feeling of independence and a changing awareness amongst women
of the period. Although the tendency is to associate women's war

employment with work in the munitions factories or on the land, the traditional homework industries of women did not totally disappear with the coming of war. During the war there were, of course, still women who, because of old age, family responsibilities or some disability, could not take up the new jobs available to them.

Whereas it is relatively easy to find out about women's war work in munitions there is little evidence to point to the fact that homework was still going on during the 1914–18 period. It is Sylvia Pankhurst's concern for working-class women and her involvement with the East End of London's working-class community that provides us with the most informative record of homework's continuing existence. Through her paper *The Woman's Dreadnought* she brought to light many injustices and grievances suffered by working-class women. Her writings clearly illustrate that the problem of sweated labour in the home did not disappear with a war economy. In fact, we are shown that the position of the woman dependent upon homework could even be worsened by the war, as seen in this letter written by a shirtmaker and printed in *The Woman's Dreadnought* in June 1914:

I can assure you that without the slightest exaggeration times are very hard for women. I, myself, have made shirts for a living, or rather a bare existence, this last twenty years, and work that I, a few years ago, received 3s. 7d. a dozen for making, I now have to do the self same work for 2s. 7d. Who is to blame? I think you know. Can you wonder we are at war, when good women are being driven to suicide, and in some cases something worse . . .[10]

The demands of the war economy also changed the type of homework available to women. Army clothing and kitbags began to make up a large percentage of homework. *The Woman's Dreadnought* brought to light recurrent examples of evidence drawing attention to the fact that government contractors were responsible for sweating homeworkers. H. D. Roberts, Chairman of the Liverpool Anti-sweating League, reported that his local experience confirmed the allegation that women making army clothing were receiving sweated rates of pay. Roberts found that women employed on kitbags and military uniforms were paid 25 per cent less than the statutory minimum as enforced by the Trade Board Act. A woman making fifty-six kitbags, stated Roberts, could hope to earn only ten shillings after deductions.[11] It would seem that not only did government contractors' rates of pay for army clothing compare unfavourably with some private employers' rates, but also the work was commonly of a more unpleasant nature. *The Woman's Dreadnought* for August 1914 reported:

> Jamesons' of Poplar, Government Contractors, pay women 2s. 1d. a dozen for making soldiers' shirts. One woman who has been making boys' shirts for 2s. 6d. a dozen, to be sold to private firms, tells us that she refused the Government work until there was no more private work to do. She tells us that the soldiers' shirts, besides being paid at lower rates, are larger and more complicated than the others, and are of harsh stuff that makes the women's fingers sore. The shirts are dark and the cotton black, and the work therefore tries the eyes a good deal. The women can only manage to do a dozen shirts a day, by working very hard and out of the 2s. 1d. they earn by this, they have to pay 2¼d. a reel for cotton – a reel does not do quite a dozen shirts. These shirts used to be sewn with thread which cost 3d. per reel but the women protested so much that they are allowed to use cotton now.
>
> For finishing the same shirts – that is sewing on buttons and making buttonholes – a Canning Town employer pays 2d. a dozen shirts . . . they can earn only 6s. or 7s. a week. They too have to find their own cotton and are obliged to do the work very much more carefully and firmly than when making shirts for ordinary wear.
>
> Strange patriotism this, that allows the Government contractors who are making money out of this War to sweat the women workers in this disgraceful fashion?[12]

Khaki cloth found its way from the direct government contractors to small towns and villages around the country and it was the unprotected and unorganised women workers who paid the highest price for this process of subcontracting. Khaki was extremely heavy and unpleasant material to work with; many homeworkers could not work on it because it was too heavy for their machines. Most of the homeworkers in the villages around Colchester made army clothing of more lightweight materials:

> They made chiefly overseas wear, shorts and so on for soldiers

overseas in tropical countries. Safari jackets and shorts it was. It wasn't the actual uniforms, not the heavy stuff they used to wear in them days. Really denims. Material for soldiers uniforms would require special machinery because it was so heavy.

But Mrs Brown had an industrial machine:

Of course I got married afterwards and my husband went into the army. Well then I still lived at home with my mother and we had all this military work – khaki. Oh dear, and wasn't that a business because it was heavy, you know. Well of course I had a big industrial machine . . . 'course I couldn't do heavy work like that on a small machine . . . earned a lot of money at that – military work . . .

My husband was a baker. Of course he was exempted for a little while but he went into the army and of course he didn't trouble to get a house then and I lived at home with my mother and I'd always done it [tailoring] and I was pleased 'cos I'd got something to do while he was away, with the baby.

Subcontracting played an important part in bringing down rates of pay for government work. It was found that the government work was being subcontracted often as many as four times. The following report appeared in *The Woman's Dreadnought* in October 1914:

The Stepney Public Health Committee has called attention to the fact that the War Office contractors in the district are only paying 2s. 9d. for making a soldier's khaki coat, 3s. 3d. for an overcoat, 10d. for a pair of trousers. The 2s. 9d. for jackets is frequently reduced to 2s. 4d. It is said that Government contracts are sometimes four times sub-let, and as each subcontractor takes a profit the women who actually do the work are ground down to the lowest point.

War Office contractors are getting rich out of the war. When will the Government prevent their shameful exploitation of poor women? Women need the vote to compel the Government to enforce decent rates of wages.[13]

Sylvia Pankhurst actively campaigned against the continuing exploitation of homeworkers and organised several exhibitions of sweated wartime labour in Caxton Hall. The aim of these exhibitions was to give people the opportunity to see for themselves the sweating of homeworkers engaged on government contracted army work. A common complaint from the homeworkers was that of insecurity of employment. It was, they said, impossible to predict when work would be available while rates of pay were also very variable.

The type of woman who was still dependent upon homework during the war is illustrated by a description of one of these exhibitions, held in 1915.[14] An example of a typical homeworker was a widow from Poplar employed in making up soldiers' trousers. She was forced into homework in order to keep herself and one dependent child. Although she worked from 5.20 am until late every night she claimed that she still would not be able to manage if it were not for the allowance she received from an adult son in the Army. This woman received only 2½d. a pair for finishing trousers. In order to earn this 2½d. she had to

> soap the bottoms of the trousers then turn the hem and fell it. She has to put in the seat linings and what is called the 'curtain' or 'back holland' also the band of lining round the top; she has to put on twelve buttons and tack and sew part of the fly. She can finish a pair of trousers in an hour, but as the day wears on her speed diminishes.
>
> Out of the 2s. 6d. a dozen pairs of trousers that she is paid for her work, she has to buy black and white cotton, soap and thread. A pennyworth of soap does twelve pairs of trousers, a threepenny reel of thread does two dozen pairs, a threepenny reel lasts a week and a half.[15]

Whereas before the war the government had passed legislation aimed at improving the situation of the homeworkers, during the war government contract work was given out at homework rates that could not but reduce women to the position of sweated labourers.

Women suffered greatly in the early stages of the war, when, with many of their traditional employments depressed, they had not yet found a foothold in alternative areas of the economy. There were, therefore, still severe cases of hardship which an inadequate system of social security benefits failed to alleviate. In December 1914, *The*

Women's Dreadnought reported that the government scale of relief in London was ten shillings for an adult and fourteen shillings for a couple, but found evidence of great fluctuations in payment.[16] The large increase in food prices during the war also helped to contribute towards hardship. Bread and potatoes formed the staple diet of the less well-off but the government took no action to curtail the escalation in price of these basics until 1917, when they finally introduced a subsidy. Thus, although the war brought new openings and entirely different life-styles for a large majority of women, for those still tied to their homes for various reasons, poverty and sweated labour continued to remain very much a part of their everyday existence. Homeworkers, as we have seen, were a hidden sector of the pre-war labour market and accounts of women's war-work detailing their employment in munitions, in transport or in agriculture provide even less of a picture of the sweated home labourer.

At the end of the First World War there were 1 086 000 women trade unionists. The war had increased women's membership by 60 per cent.[17] In 1918, as a direct result of their participation in the war effort, women over thirty years of age were granted the vote. These developments, combined with the opening of doors into a whole host of employments previously barred to women, surely marked the arrival of a new political and socio-economic status for women in society? Unfortunately not; women were not allowed to reap the full benefits of their war experience. The country was no longer in an extraordinary situation of war but had returned to the normality of peacetime, so women had to return to their 'normal' place in society. During the war women workers in field and factory were not 'unwomanly' but patriotic: in the name of patriotism women were encouraged to perform so-called 'men's work'. The 'return to normal' meant that women had to return uncomplainingly to their homes and traditional areas of employment while the men, upon returning to a 'land fit for heroes' attempted to reclaim their old jobs. The attitude of the time is captured in this extract from the *Daily Graphic*:

> The idea that because the state called for women to help the nation, the state must continue to employ them is too absurd for sensible women to entertain. As a matter of grace, notice should be at least a fortnight and if possible a month. As for young

women formerly in domestic service, they at least should have no difficulty in finding vacancies.[18]

The trade union movement itself was instrumental in exerting pressure that resulted in women's dismissal from 'men's jobs', in particular in engineering, transport and printing. In the first few months after the war almost 50 per cent of previously employed women found themselves out of work or on short time. The view that certain types of employment were inherently unsuitable for women was forcefully reasserted. It is difficult to generalise but it is likely that many women were sad at having to give up their war work and the companionship that went with it. However, to speak against the displacement of women to enable the return of the men to their former jobs would no doubt have been condemned as totally unpatriotic. The following reminiscence, in which Molly Weir describes the feelings of her mother at having to surrender her war time work, captures something of the mood of the time:

> Before taking this job in the paint-shop she had worked a machine at Hyde Park, where they made the big locomotives. She was very proud of her skill with the strong steel shapes, and sad when they had to sack all the women workers to make room for the men who needed the jobs. They made no fuss, the widows, at being ousted in this way. They accepted the fact that in normal conditions man was the breadwinner, and quietly looked elsewhere for work.[19]

The pre-war values and mores about the role and status of men and women in society were reasserted with some vehemence and women who were not in full agreement were unlikely to have found the confidence or indeed the opportunity to make their voices heard. Within a year of the Armistice, three-quarters of a million women had been dismissed.

What were the significant long-term developments in women's employment during the period covering the First World War and the inter-war years? There had been a rapid population increase in the nineteenth century. During the inter-war years the population was still rising but at a somewhat lower rate: the population of England and Wales was 36 071 000 in 1911, 37 887 000 in 1921 and 39 952 000 in 1931. There was a shift in population growth from the traditional industrial centres to the South-East and the Midlands. In 1931 the population was predominantly urban, with only 30 per cent living in rural areas. About a quarter of the urban population was living in London.[20]

The composition of the population was also changing. Whereas the ratio of females to males had been 1068:1000 in 1911, it was 1096:1000 in 1921 and 1088:1000 in 1931. This increased imbalance between the sexes after the First World War meant that fewer women could hope to marry, and a decline in family size also took place between the beginning of the century and the Second World War. The fall in the birth-rate reached its lowest level in 1933, but there was also a decline in the infant mortality rate. Although the decline in average family size meant that parents were responsible for a smaller number of children, the exclusion of children from the labour market meant an extended period of dependency on parents. A further important demographic change was the increasing longevity of the population. In 1911 and 1921 persons over sixty-five years of age made up 5 per cent of the population, but by 1931 this had increased to 6 per cent. Old-age pensions were introduced in 1911. This state support meant that although a larger number of the population were reaching old age they were no longer totally dependent upon their children for support at this stage of their life and a large family was no longer seen as security for old age.

The inter-war years witnessed an economic slump in the staple heavy industries but also the growth of new industries such as motor vehicle manufacture. There was a decline in the numbers employed in the old traditional industries of agriculture, mining, textiles and metal-working, and an increase in commerce, personal service, public administration, entertainment and manufacture of food, drink and tobacco. This was a time for the development of light industries and for a transition from emphasis on the production of goods to the production of services. New industrial centres grew up in the South. Despite the depression in the old industrial centres, the standard of living for the working class was rising slowly in the South and East during the inter-war years.

The development of light industries and the growth in retailing meant increasing employment opportunities for women and there was a big increase in the number of women employed in the non-manual occupations. An informative account of changes in this area is to be found in *The New Survey of London Life and Labour*.[21] This was an attempt to explore broadly similar areas of London's social and economic life as those which had been looked at by Charles Booth in his mammoth survey of some forty years earlier. However, the 1930 survey also embraced urban boroughs outside the county of London in an attempt to reproduce as closely as possible the type of area covered by Booth.[22] Unfortunately, no continuous comparable chain of statistics was available over the forty-year period but the New Survey makes use of census returns and statistics of Unemployment Insurance. Whereas Booth's 'poverty line' has been 21s. the *New Survey* equivalent was estimated at 40s.

By far the most extensive change to be recorded in the *New Survey* was the advance in the development of mechanisation and subsequent decline in work done by hand.[23] One consequence of this development was to open more areas of employment to women as there was an increased division of labour and a growth in less skilled and more repetitive work. Mechanisation also meant less casual employment was available.

As in 1890, the clothing industry continued to be the main field of employment for women after the domestic occupations: women were especially prominent in dressmaking, millinery and shirt-making. In these branches of clothing the *New Survey* recorded nine out of ten workers as female.[24] In 1921 the clothing trades as a whole were employing 200 000 workers in Greater London and two-thirds of these were women.[25] The main change since Booth's time had been the development of the clothing industry from the handicraft stage to one of greater mechanisation: the seamstress had practically disappeared. By 1930 no woman could be legally employed in the London clothing trades for less than 7d. an hour or an equivalent of 28s. for a forty-eight hour week. Differentials based on sex were still rampant and the male rate was 11½d. an hour or 46s. for a forty-eight hour week.[26] However, it would appear that it was the female workers in the clothing trades that received the largest proportional increases in wage rates resulting from the Trade Boards Act.

Domestic service and clothing may have remained the largest employers of female labour but the greatest proportional increases in female employment were in distribution, hotels and catering and in various service trades. The 1870 Education Act facilitated the movement of women into new and expanding areas of employment. By 1900 the majority of adult women were literate and better equipped for a wider variety of jobs. The years up to the First World War and the inter-war period witnessed the increased employment of women in shops, commerce and to a lesser extent in the professions. Clerical and commercial work opened up a new field of 'respectable' female employment. Office work was seen as more genteel than factory work and of higher status than shop work. The majority of office workers were single women; as in so many instances the choice was between marriage and a job, although the majority of office jobs for women could not be seen as leading to a career. Many employers dismissed women upon marriage and in the context of the mass unemployment of the inter-war period the fertile soil was there in which to re-establish the pre-war seeds of prejudice against women working and in particular against married women working.

Despite improved employment opportunities, the mass unemployment and Depression years of the 1920s and 1930s did much to erode women's new industrial status: they were forced back into the lowest-paid jobs including the most traditional female occupation of all, domestic service. The Means Test played an active part in this process. Women tended to receive even harsher treatment than men and those who refused to accept any kind of work offered to them immediately found their benefit stopped. It was reported in 1927 that one East End of London labour exchange stopped the benefit of fifty women in one week while the *Ministry of Labour Gazette* stated that five thousand women had been removed from the books in one month, the majority on the charge of 'not genuinely seeking work'.[27] The introduction of the Anomalies Regulations affected the right of married women to claim benefit. Those women who had not paid any contributions since marriage were not to receive benefit.[28]

Many factories were once again refusing to employ married women and they were forced to resort to their traditional casual extended domestic occupations such as taking in lodgers and going out cleaning. Domestic service had suffered a fall in recruitment as a result of the First World War but the Depression years and the Means Test encouraged the replenishment of the supply of servants.

The shortage of servants in the early 1920s had been considered a serious problem by the servant-employing strata of society and by 1923 the worry concerning the supply of domestic servants was seen as sufficient to warrant an investigation. The object of a Ministry-of-Labour-appointed committee was to enquire into 'present conditions as to the supply of domestic servants and in particular into the effect of the Unemployment Insurance Scheme in this connection.'[29] Lack of alternative work forced young girls back to domestic service and helped to revive the 'living-in' system that the war had done so much to erode.[30] Girls were even transferred to the areas where there was a demand for domestic servants. Although the living-in system for shop assistants had also suffered a real decline, shop work was an ever-expanding area of employment for the single female. It had much in common with domestic service, as was noted in the *New Survey of London Life and Labour*:

> There is a link, which is not first apparent, that is between shop workers and the domestic service group. The personal service they have to give, waiting on the needs and perhaps whims of others, brings them nearer to this group than they would care to admit.[31]

By 1931 over two million women and girls were employed in the 'personal service' type occupations.

With the increase in respectable jobs it had become much more the norm for single women to go out to work and a spirit of emancipation was evident in certain circles as young single women sought independence in office or shop work. However, as the Second World War drew nearer it became obvious that women were still confined to the worst-paid sectors of the economy. This was made possible by the continued designation of a category of employment as 'women's work'. In 1921, 33 per cent of women were in domestic service, 12 per cent in textiles, 11 per cent in clothing, 9 per cent were shop assistants and 5 per cent were clerks.

Married women's employment outside the home was still very much dependent upon the traditions of an area and hence remained a predominantly urban phenomenon concentrated in and around Lancashire and the Midlands. It became an increasingly widespread assumption that a man's wages should be sufficient to support a wife and children as dependants and working-class respectability was very dependent upon the wife not going out to work. The single woman was gaining a wider experience of life through economic changes and educational developments both of which gave her a greater independence, but this new independence was severely curtailed with marriage when a woman was seen both by the state and by the working class itself, to become totally dependent upon the male breadwinner. Whereas 25 per cent of married women worked in 1851 and 13 per cent at the turn of the century, only 12 per cent were working in 1921 and this downward trend was not revised until after the Second World War. Most married women could not work outside the home except in the capacity of charwomen and the majority of single women were once again firmly entrenched in an area of the economy designated as 'women's work'.[32]

Many were still struggling to pick up the pieces from the ravages of the First World War when they were hit by the Depression years of the 1920s and 1930s. There was hardly one family that had not suffered a bereavement. The number of widows with dependent children had increased and many more women had to face a life without a husband. It was a period remembered more for the suffering and hardship brought by unemployment rather than for new employment opportunities. In 1931, 2·7 million were unemployed. Unemployment Insurance Benefit for an adult male in 1931 was 17s. a week, 9s. for his dependent wife and 2s. for each child. An insured unemployed woman received only 15s. a week.

But certain improvements had taken place since the nineteenth century: the population was generally healthier; educational opportunities were greater; the school leaving age had been raised to fourteen years and there were visible improvements in housing, with slum-clearance programmes. However, as numerous social enquiries revealed, a large percentage of the population were still living in poverty. Seebohm Rowntree's 1936 study of York, *Poverty and Progress*, showed that illness, old age, low wages and unemployment were still major causes of poverty. In particular, the young and old were suffering. Malnutrition and ill-health affected many of the working class, but especially women, who were the first to make sacrifices when money was short. Many houses were still grossly overcrowded. The Means Test was considered a great evil which caused much resentment and hardship.

The state came to play a greater role than ever before through such Ministries as Health, Labour and Pensions and central government had taken over certain functions previously considered to be the sole concern of the family. However, despite the development of the Welfare State many families remained under nourished, ill-clothed, badly housed and in poor health.

Changing trade conditions and the greater economic efficiency of mechanisation brought an end to homework in a variety of trades. The invention of new machinery and increasing subdivision of labour within the factory often made homework seem an inefficient proposition. In many firms and industries homework was a traditional form of production but as new industries or processes were developed it was no longer automatically included as a method in the production process.

By the time of the inter-war period many processes that had previously been regarded as predominantly home industries had been transferred back to the factory. Women workers continued to predominate in the clothing industries but much of their work was transferred to factories. Nevertheless, the clothing industries still continued to employ the greatest number of homeworkers. The *New Survey* continued in Booth's tradition and divided outworkers into two main categories. The most skilled worker was still prevalent in the West End trade. He was usually male and rarely employed other members of his family. The unskilled worker, most commonly the married woman, the elderly or disabled, continued the tradition of East End homework catering to the demand for the cheapest grades of work. By the time of the New Survey this latter group were working mainly at machining and finishing. An investigation of sixty female homeworkers in East and North London showed most of them to be working at these two processes.[33] The majority were working alone, with only seven employing 'assistants': in four cases the assistant was a daughter; in two a sister; and in only one instance a person from outside the family. In twelve cases they did all the work involved in making the garment – seven of these were in vest-making. Twenty-one women machined women's coats and costumes and four worked on ready-made trousers. Twenty-two women worked at 'finishing', with eighteen of them working on ready-made trousers, two on women's coats, one on men's coats and one on retail bespoke trousers. The women were divided into three groups according to marital status: thirty-three were married with husbands, twelve were widows and fourteen were single. All except one of the single women were entirely dependent upon their own earnings for a livelihood. Some of the widows were in receipt of pensions. Out of the thirty-three married women, twenty-nine of the husbands were in employment, two in receipt of pensions and one temporarily unemployed. Perhaps the percentage of single women is slightly higher than we might expect: this is not the case, however, if we take into account the shortage of alternative employment in 1929 and perhaps the return to the belief that work inside the home was, in terms of respectability, preferable to certain outside employment. The single women received higher earnings and were the group of women in the sample who regarded homework as a full-time occupation. For example, nearly half the single women earned over 25s. a week, whereas for half of the married women earnings ranged from 15s. to 22s. 6d.

The *New Survey* sample surveys of homeworkers revealed that a representative type of homeworker was a middle-aged married woman. She was often married to an unskilled labourer earning £2–£3 a week. Her work, they concluded, supplemented the family wage and helped to provide a better standard of living. The casual employment of men had previously been a driving force for women to take in homework; however, from the 1890s the regularity in the supply of work increased in many areas of the economy. There was an overall decline in the demand for casual work in modern industry – for example, by 1930, work in the docks, a notorious area for low pay and casual labour, was in more regular supply and the minimum wage of the London docker was 12s. for an eight-hour day. Thus one significant change was the disappearance of male casual work as an important motivating force for married women taking in homework.

Homeworkers retained the character of a casual labour pool for the clothing industry. They were still an important part of the labour force as the industry continued to be subject to seasonal fluctuations in demand. The *New Survey* estimated the number of homeworkers in London as being between 3500 and 5000 in tailoring, 1000 in dressmaking, 300 in shirtmaking and 500 in tie-making.[34] Dressmaking and women's underclothing embraced a large variety of garments – women and children's non-tailored outer garments, undergarments and baby linen. Of the 57 000 workers employed in London in 1929, 95 percent were women and girls,[35] and dressmaking continued to employ a significant number of homeworkers in both the wholesale and retail branch of the trade. The majority of homeworkers made garments throughout, whether or not it was machine or hand work. Finishing was also an important occupation. The garments worked on by homeworkers at this time included blouses, dresses, jumpers, dressing gowns, nightdresses, pyjamas, belts, overalls, knickers, petticoats, scarves, shawls and children's frocks and coats.[36] The *New Survey*'s sample investigation of homeworkers in 'dressmaking' showed that the majority had previously been employed as indoor hands. About half the women were found to be single, and in the majority of cases the homeworker was solely dependent upon her own earnings.[37] Homeworkers were also still to be found in the boot and shoe industry but women worked mainly on children's shoes and slippers.

Changes in fashion were responsible for the decline in certain homework trades. For example, the *New Survey* recorded a noticeable decline in corset-making, which had previously employed a significant number of homeworkers. This was certainly due to a change in fashion, as was the decline in feather dressing.[38] The artificial-flower-making trade had also previously been an important employer of homeworkers but by 1930 it had greatly declined. This decline could again be blamed on fashion, with the millinery trade no longer making the same demand for artificial flowers as it had in Booth's time. Artificial flowers continued to be used for decorative and charitable purposes but the homeworker lost her place in this industry to the factory worker and ex-serviceman. In fact, the British Legion was active in encouraging an expansion in homework: ex-servicemen under the guidance of the British Legion were involved in making-up articles to be sold in their shops and at their various fund-raising occasions. This was undoubtedly a new development in homeworking and was a direct result of the First World War. The *New Survey* recorded a decline in the number of middlemen involved in distributing homework in clothing. The distribution process varied, with work sometimes being given out by a subcontractor and sometimes delivered straight from the ready-made clothes factory or another homeworker.

There were few developments in the field of legislation *vis-à-vis* homework during the period between the first Trade Boards Act and the Second World War. However, more and more trades came under the sway of the trade boards during this period and it seems that these helped to hasten the decline of homework in industries such as matchbox-making. The *New Survey* estimate was that about two-thirds of the workers in London industries coming under the Trade Board Acts were women and girls.[39] However, as we have seen, the trade boards did not eradicate the demand for homeworkers in all industries. The New Survey concluded that:

> Many of the 'sweated' industries of Charles Booth's day are now governed by Trade Boards, but even in these trades the growth of factories, and the pressure of the minimum wage have not caused the disappearance of the small workshop or the homeworker, though generally speaking the proportion of the total production carried out by these methods has greatly diminished.[40]

Inevitably, the Trade Board Acts were a factor that employers were forced to take into account in assessing the value of homeworkers. The trade boards could also militate against the homeworker herself in that they encouraged employers to dismiss their slower workers. Employers, by speeding up their factory workers, for example through the introduction of more efficient machinery and piece-work incentives, could increase productivity and perhaps eradicate the need for homeworkers altogether.

In many trades homework did decline or disappear during the first quarter of this century and Trade Boards no doubt played a part in this decline. However, a noticeable exception was the continuing demand for homework in branches of the clothing trades. In reference to this the *New Survey* has the following comment to make:

> There is no doubt that in most trades homework has greatly diminished in recent years. It is more commonly the concomitant of small-scale workshop production than of factory industry and generally speaking it diminishes as factory methods develop. A doubt is suggested . . . whether there has in fact been a diminution of homework in tailoring, but it is to be remembered that tailoring is the branch of clothing in which the small unit of production has been most persistent.[41]

In certain branches of the clothing industry and in particular in tailoring, there is no doubt that the decline in homeworking was retarded by a shortage of indoor labour. The 1912 Committee on Outworkers quoted the representative of the National Federation of Merchant Tailors as stating that, 'In the busy seasons we cannot get the workshops filled . . . We should prefer to have the whole thing indoors, but we cannot get the labour so we have to resort to the outdoor worker.'[42] The seasonality in demand and fluctuations in fashion continued to make the homeworker an important component of the labour force in the clothing industries. Therefore one of the chief characteristics of homework remained – that is, unpredictability in the supply of work. Homeworkers continued to be used to help employers cope with seasonal and surprise demands for goods and consequently they still suffered from total job insecurity. Little had changed to improve the situation of the homeworker by the time of the inter-war period.

We can conclude, therefore, that as far as the inter-war period is concerned, homework had declined but not disappeared. It remained prevalent not only throughout the clothing trades – homeworkers still carded hooks, eyes and buttons, made artificial flowers, Christmas cards and crackers, brushes, lamp shades, tea cosies and pincushions, mended nets, worked in upholstery, caned chair seats and so on. But homework, along with other forms of casual work, certainly came to play a smaller part in the twentieth-century economy than it had done during the second half of the nineteenth century. In the 1925 Annual Report of the Chief Inspector of Factories and Workshops it was claimed that an examination of the lists of homeworkers kept by employers gave a definite impression of a decrease in the number of homeworkers being employed when compared to pre-war lists. This was also, stated the Report, backed up by enquiries from local authorities. The 1925 Report concluded that there was:

Not much room for casual work in modern industry; moreover, outwork in the past has not usually been well organised and it has been difficult to secure that the work has been properly done and delivered at the right time. Formerly these disadvantages were probably counteracted by the cheapness of this form of labour, but the development of the trade boards has removed that advantage.[43]

The Report is perhaps guilty of making too sweeping a generalisation in its conclusion. The attraction of employing homeworkers has never been completely eradicated and certainly in 1925 a number of employers could still see that there were benefits to be had in employing what was, in spite of the trade boards, a very cheap and plentiful reservoir of labour.

The relative silence and absence of any signs of concern over homework from any pressure group and in particular from the trade union movement during the inter-war period no doubt helps to create the impression that homework had all but disappeared. However, it was very likely that homework would fade into the background as the trade union movement of the inter-war period was dominated by such great industrial struggles as the 1926 General Strike and the mass unemployment of the period. Occasional references, during the inter-war years, to homework can still be found amongst the papers of the trade union movement but they are few and far between. Not surprisingly, it is in the clothing unions that the most persistent record of continuing concern over homework is to be found. For example, in 1924, Mr Bernard Sullivan, London organiser of the Tailor and Garment Workers Union, was to be found voicing an old concern about homework:

The great obstacle to organising in the City is the outworker . . . The people in the factories say that the low rate and bad conditions of the outworker make it harder for them to get and maintain proper conditions and they urge us to deal with the condition of the outworker.[44]

In general, homework received only localised and spasmodic interest from the trade union movement of the period stretching from the first Trade Boards Act up to the resurgence of interest in the 1970s.

Another reason for the overall decline in homework was a fall in the demand for this work by the women themselves. More areas of male employment began to provide work of a regular rather than a casual nature and there were also slight improvements in wages. As the earnings of the chief wage earner increase in relation to the cost of living the economic need for the 'extra' earnings of his wife diminishes. The extent and type of casual work women were prepared to undertake changed in relation to changes taking place in the working-class male's economic status in certain strata of Victorian society and a decline in the supply of women wanting to take on homework occurred. The same decline is also reflected in women's willingness to take on casual agricultural work. From the 1890s less field work was being done by women and by this time the agricultural gang system was virtually extinct. Improved transport also meant that workers in rural communities were not isolated from the industrial centres to the same extent and there was therefore less need for women to take in homework and less need for employers to seek out the reserve of female labour located in the non-industrial communities. It is also likely that there was less demand from younger women for homework as a wider range of jobs became available to them.

However, the Depression years of the inter-war period with their mass unemployment did much to reverse the situation. Wives and daughters were forced to fall back on traditional female occupations because husbands, fathers and brothers were often unemployed for years at a time, so homework once again became a sought-after employment.

The mobilisation for the war was at its peak at the end of 1943. In the middle of 1944 there were 17·25 million women of working age in Great Britain: of these 7 650 000 were in the women's services, in industry, or in the full-time civil defence. About one million were in the Women's Voluntary Service.[45] In 1943 two out of five (or 40 per cent) of all married women were in paid employment, compared with only one in seven in 1939. Married women were the major source of untapped labour that could be directed into the war effort. Initially, however, the government showed some reluctance to direct married women into waged work; the belief that they were responsible solely for household duties was still strong. However, as the war progressed married women became the only remaining reserve of labour. At the beginning of the Second World War, as in the previous Great War, both single and married women experienced an increase in employment but as the war dragged on they became an indispensable sector of the labour force and the war effort as a whole.

Those women suffering poverty did not, of course, need government directives to push them into the labour force. As always there were those women who needed to work in order to survive and support dependants. Allowances paid to rank-and-file servicemen were so low that they provided a major incentive for women to go out to work. Allowances were often lower than what had been previously earned by the male breadwinner and this, coupled with the rise in the cost of living, often meant a fall in the family income. Many women were forced out to work even though the government did argue that, for example, a woman with young children need not work full-time. It was those women who had few options open to them who took on the most gruelling and arduous war work. Those who had to be persuaded to go out to work, in conflict with the ideal of innate feminine domesticity that they claimed to espouse, the women of the middle and upper classes, often took up voluntary work or less arduous war work more in keeping with their social position.[46]

The government's initial hesitancy to involve married women in waged work stemmed from the traditional fear that to remove women from their 'natural' place was to risk creating a potential threat to stability and the status quo. There was particular concern about the possible effect on the morale of the men in the work-force and in the services. Women with domestic responsibilities and older women were the very last to be brought into the labour force by the government.

The domestic ideology by no means disappeared with the war; it was merely adapted and used to meet the changed conditions: women were urged to make use of their domestic talents and housewifely skills in order to further the war effort. The work of the housewife became more visible and received an acknowledgement that was missing in normal peace-time conditions. Housewives were encouraged to play their part in the war effort by not wasting food, by conjuring up new dishes out of limited war rations and by make-do-and-mend. The burden of domestic work increased with the new problems of rationing, shortages and long queues for food. Many women found that their domestic duties had extended to embrace a number of other activities such as letter-writing, acting as surrogate mother to child evacuees, or performing domestic work for adults who were billeted on them. Psychological stress was obviously much greater with lengthy family separations, the threat and reality of bereavements, and loneliness.

The war required a different emphasis and different standards, but domestic work and the role of the housewife was, if anything, more crucial than ever in maintaining social stability and the status quo. The war highlighted the importance of domestic labour to the smooth running of capitalist society. The figure of the housewife was central to the war effort and during the Second World War many women came to see the combining of marriage and children with wage work as a natural state. However, any watering-down of the main tenets of domestic ideology were consistently viewed as temporary expedients by the government to deal with an extraordinary situation. As the end of the war came in sight women with domestic responsibilities – a husband and children – were the first to be released from the obligation to work. As after the First World War, married women were expected to forget their war experience and return to a state of normality exemplified by domesticity. By the end of 1946 there were 875 000 more working women than there had been in 1939.

However, the return to domesticity was not to be as total as it had been after the First World War. It became more common to combine marriage with paid employment and the number of married women in the labour force increased after the Second World War.

9

Homework, 1945–1985

After the Second World War many women were forced out of their war-time employment but the economic difficulties of the 1950s produced a scarcity of labour in specific areas of the economy and between 1951 and 1971 the labour force rose by 1.5 million to nearly 25 million. All but 69 000 of this increase was due to the employment of women.[1] The changes are illustrated in Table 9.1.[2]

Table 9.1 *Changes in the labour force, 1931–73*

	Percentage of total labour force	
	Male	*Female*
1931	70	30
1951	68	32
1968	65	35
1973	63	37

The main reason for this change was an increase in the number of women working outside the home. In 1931 the proportion of married women working was only 10 per cent but by 1951 it had risen to 22 per cent and by 1971 was 42 per cent. To a great extent the increase in married women's employment was due to the post-war creation of flexible shift work and part-time labour which allowed married women to perform both domestic and waged labour. In 1951 there were 784 000 female part-time workers and in 1971 there were 2 749 000, or about a third of the total female labour force. Part-time work has always been especially prevalent in the low-paying sectors of the economy which employ large numbers of women: these include clothing, catering, the food and drink industries, shops, laundries and the National Health Service.

Changes in the birth-rate, marriage age and the changing demands of the post-war economy all contributed to women's greater participation in the labour force. As women had fewer children a shorter part of their lives was given over to childbearing and childrearing. As women finished childbearing at an earlier age and as their life expectancy increased many more women were able and willing to return to waged work. In 1974 women workers over forty years of age made up nearly half of all female employees. However, the full participation of women in the labour force was inhibited by practical difficulties such as the lack of childcare facilities and by the continued emphasis placed on the evils of the 'working mother'. The latter belief was strengthened by the work of John Bowlby and his emphasis on the claim that the separation of a child from its mother in the first five years of life could do it irreparable damage. The Bowlby legacy proved a tenacious one: in 1971, 58 per cent of married women without dependent children worked more than thirty hours a week compared to only 30 per cent of those with two dependent children.[3]

Domestic work and childcare continued to be seen as primarily the responsibility of women and continued to determine the range of jobs available to them in the post-war period. Despite the fact that in 1975 there were about nine million women workers only one-third were to be found in manufacturing industries while the rest were concentrated in the service sector. The major employers of women since the Second World War were distribution (shops), the professional and scientific sector (nursing and teaching for example), and the miscellaneous service industries (catering, laundries and so on). Women's labour outside the home therefore continued to mirror her work in the home: the majority of female employment involved the servicing of people's immediate needs. Only a small number of women were to be found in jobs that involved skills or training totally unconnected with domestic labour. The mass increase in the numbers of women in the labour market since the Second World War did not involve the majority in forms of employment that would conflict with traditional notions about women's domesticity.

The number of skilled jobs available to women declined during this century. Between 1911 and 1951 the number of women categorised as skilled in industry fell by about a third and between 1951 and 1961 by a further 8.5 per cent.[4] One large area of female employment where the element of skill was destroyed by modernisation was shop work, with the growth of self-service and large supermarkets. The largest group of skilled female workers were secretaries and typists: in 1971 there were 737 000 of these, and only 1.4 per cent were men. However, despite its categorisation as skilled work, the secretary or typist was most often employed by a male boss for whom she was expected to run errands and make coffee; these tasks may not have been part of the job description but they were services which many bosses took for granted as part of 'women's work'.

Despite improved educational opportunities, relatively few women were found in management or the professions – teaching was the only profession that employed women in substantial numbers. Even in occupations or industries where women far outnumbered men, such as clothing, retailing and food production, only a small number were found in managerial or supervisory positions. Promotion was rare for women even when they did manage to force their way into occupations with a definite career structure and promotional ladder. For example, in 1975, women doctors made up 27 per cent of the total but only 12 per cent of consultants. During the 1973-4 11 per cent of university teachers and research staff were women but only, 1.7 per cent of professors were female.[5]

Women continued to be badly paid relative to their male colleagues. Between 1950 and 1970 women's weekly earnings as a percentage of men's fell from 55 per cent to 51 per cent.[6] The concentration of women into specific occupational categories meant low pay remained the norm for a female work-force. Textiles, clothing and footwear all employed a large female labour force and were amongst the lowest paying of all the manufacturing industries. In 1975 nearly 10 per cent of the labour force came under the auspices of a wages council.[7] Wages council industries were some of the lowest paid in the country and included clothing, retail and distribution, hairdressing, laundries and catering. Trade unions found it difficult to reach many of these low-paid women workers, especially those in industries such as hotels and catering which had a high labour turnover.

Since the Second World War, therefore, despite a massive increase in women's employment, a sexual division of labour continued to prevail in the labour market:

Women's employment has continued to be concentrated in a small number of industries and confined to a range of jobs which might be described as 'women's work'. Even where women work alongside men, they usually hold positions of lower responsibility and perform tasks of a less skilled nature . . . men are the employers, managers, top professionals, foremen and skilled workers in our society.[8]

In the 1980s the situation of women in the labour force is largely unchanged. Women remain confined to low-paid, low-status jobs with high insecurity and low job satisfaction. The twin ideals, discussed earlier, of domestic ideology and the family wage are still prevalent although they increasingly fly in the face of reality of most women's lives.

In spite of the equal pay and sex discrimination legislation of the mid-1970s, the position of women is worse now in the 1980s than it was in the 1970s. In an economic recession with a government committed to cutbacks in the public sector, women are hit badly: they are the ones who lose their jobs first, who suffer from the lack of nursery facilities and cutbacks in expenditure on health and education.

Women remain employed predominantly in the service industries. More than three-quarters of all female workers are in the non-productive sector of the work-force and women are still confined to specific industries within each sector. Half of all women in the productive sector are in four industries: food and drink, clothing and footwear, textiles, and electrical engineering. More than half of all women workers are caterers, cleaners, hairdressers, nurses or secretaries. So although the days are gone when marriage was expected to lift women out of the labour market, women have only been drawn into the world of paid work in a handful of occupations and industries.[9] There is a staggering degree of segregation within the work-force. In 1980, 45 per cent of women and about 75 per cent of men worked in totally segregated jobs.[10]

A major change in women's work has come about with the microchip technology, which can replace many of the unskilled and semi-skilled jobs normally done by women, above all in clerical and secretarial work.[11] It remains to be seen what its impact will be on secretaries and shorthand-typists but it seems clear that increased automation will cause unemployment in these sectors.

Contrary to popular belief, homework did not disappear with the end of the inter-war Depression years and the growth in strength and influence of a national trade union movement. Certainly the homeworker of the post-Second World War period has been no more visible than her sister of the earlier period. The Trade Boards Act and the First World War brought an end to the campaign to improve the situation of homeworkers. Trade unionists no doubt felt that there were other more pressing issues on which to campaign. Occasional newspaper reports and comments by trade unionists in industries particularly affected by homework show that the homework system persisted under modern economic conditions. In 1948, James Crawford, President of the National Union of Boot and Shoe Operatives, voiced the old grievances against homework: 'It disrupts the home, adversely affects children – in some cases it involves them in assisting the parents in the making of bows and ornaments – and evades completely the Factory Acts and regulations protecting the employment of women and young children.'[12]

Crawford estimated that in one shoe centre alone there were 600–700 homeworkers and in another two centres a total of 700, while in the hosiery industry there were 12000 homeworkers.[13] In 1953, union complaints were again being voiced against homework in the boot and shoe industry. The majority of homeworkers in the industry were married women machining the uppers of shoes and slippers. The union had agreed to the use of a homework labour force at a time when there had been a shortage of machinists in the industry. Robert Driver, secretary of the Rossendale Union of Boot, Shoe and Slipper Operatives complained that many homeworkers were working 'at all hours' including Saturdays, Sundays and holidays:

> These outworkers who have to be union members were not allowed until after the War. The original idea was that they should be women who need to stay at home. If a person is able to come to the factory at all we want her to do so, even on a part time basis. We have some control over operatives in a factory but none in the home.[14]

This is an interesting statement because it illustrates the persistence of homework in a particular industry and shows the continuing failure of trade unions to influence a scattered and isolated homeworking labour force.

Evidence that the numbers of homeworkers was again increasing after the Second World War was also provided by another union greatly concerned with the homeworker, the National Union of Tailor and Garment Workers (NUTGW). In 1955, Miss Maycock, chairwoman of the NUTGW, voiced criticism of the system of homeworking in the clothing industry:

> The number who are making up garments in their own homes, or on premises for which the employer makes no provision, is well nigh three to four times greater than before the War. I say without hesitation these women are being employed in their homes only because their labour is cheap . . . Taken as a whole the system of homeworking represents a menace to the standards of employment of the indoor worker.[15]

At their 1957 Conference the NUTGW passed a motion to investigate homeworking in the clothing trade. Not surprisingly there was a divergence of opinion within the Union itself. One official said that the Union should reject homeworkers altogether. Another argued that homeworkers could not be ignored: there were, he said, 63 746 in England alone, of whom only 48 000 were making clothes.[16]

The divergence of opinion within the trade union movement as a whole has meant that no cohesive national policy regarding homeworkers has been formulated and fought for in the period since the Second World War. Indeed, very little publicity was given to homework for many years and so it appeared that it was a thing of the past. It was left to pressure groups rather than trade unionists to alert society to the fact that homework was far from being eradicated and a revival of interest and concern about homework occurred in the mid-1970s. Since then a number of publications and investigations have once more focused attention on the homeworker and sweated labour.[17] However, the numbers employed as homeworkers in the 1980s is still unknown. The collection and collation of statistics has remained unreliable and erratic, complicated by a lack of generally accepted definition of the term, the high labour turnover and the clandestine nature of much home industry.

Homework in the 1980s encompasses a wide variety of industries and a multitude of work processes. The bulk is still in the clothing industry, involving machining and finishing, but many other traditional home industries have also survived including the making of artificial flowers and leaves, grading and sizing pins and needles for packets, carding and boxing hair grips or slides, pairing shoelaces, painting Christmas decorations, making up Christmas crackers, painting and assembling toys and ornaments, knitting and shoe work. More recent homework occupations include electrical component assembly, the inspection and packaging of a wide range of goods, and many clerical tasks including typing, addressing envelopes, punching computer cards and collating survey data. Advances in technology have made possible the introduction of a number of new home industries. Many processes have been simplified thereby allowing the movement of a number of clerical tasks from the office to the home and it seems that this trend is likely to continue as a means of reducing costs. Technological advances in the future, with the widespread use of electronic office equipment, will make it economically viable to transfer an increasing number of work tasks to the home. In fact, an overall increase in homeworking has taken place in recent years. One union reported: 'We are convinced that homeworking is growing, particularly as many women with the necessary skills have been made redundant from factories and can only find paid employment by working at home.'[18]

During the present economic recession, increasing use is being made of what has been termed a 'marginal labour force'. Employers are keen to move over as far as possible to a more flexible work-force which today draws heavily upon part-timers, homeworkers, temporary workers and government-subsidised trainees. Homeworkers thus form part of a secondary or peripheral labour force which is characterised by low pay, lack of unionisation and few employment rights. The last few years have witnessed an increase in casual work (for example, in the National Health Service and ancillary services), an increase in part-time work (for example, in catering and retailing), and an increase in sweating (for example, in homeworking, hotels and cleaning).[19] Women have tended to be concentrated in this marginal labour force.

. Women's marginal relationship to production is perhaps nowhere better illustrated than in the clothing industry, which has the highest concentration of female workers, part-time workers and ethnic minority groups in the manufacturing sector.[20] About 80 per cent of the total labour force in clothing are women. Whereas in 1948 half a million people were employed in clothing, today the figure is under a quarter of a million.[21] However, it also employs 36 700 part timers and 8800 homeworkers. In addition, it has been estimated that as many as half of all the jobs in the London clothing industry are not officially registered.[22] The clothing industry has remained a labour-intensive industry; it has always depended on cheap labour to keep production costs down. Today, with the economic recession and foreign competition, homeworkers and sweatshops are still an integral part of clothing production. Within the industry itself, a process of de-skilling has taken place and 'women are drawn into production as cheap labour and in competition with men'.[23]

Women are employed mainly as machinists and their low wages are justified by the way machining is designated unskilled work. Employers have been able to argue this since it is a 'skill' that women often acquire at home as part of their traditional domestic work in the same way as hand-sewing was learnt in the nineteenth century and recognition has seldom been given to skills learnt at home such as knitting and sewing. Gender divisions within the clothing industry have also been accepted by male trade unionists in attempts to hold on to their 'skilled' jobs and higher wages. This sexual division of labour within the work-force has resulted from employers' determination to treat female labour as cheap labour and this has been reinforced by male insistence on their wage differentials.[24] Although the clothing industry is dominated by female labour, it is the minority of male workers who have held on to the small percentage of skilled and better-paid jobs. This occupational segregation meant that in 1976 92 per cent of women but only 36 per cent of men in the clothing industry received low wages.[25]

While there has been a general increase in women's employment, especially married women's employment, the increase in homework reflects a trend towards the 'ghettoisation' of women's labour. The belief that the man is the breadwinner and the woman works for pin-money still persists and has reinforced occupational segregation and hence wage differentials: this belief continues despite the evidence that contradicts its assumptions. For example, a study of homeworkers in Leicester showed that 'The women's earnings were an essential part of the household income. 70 per cent spent their wages on children's clothes, household items and bills'.[26]

Women's economic marginality as part-timers and homeworkers is also reflected in their employment status. The majority of homeworkers are self-employed. This means that they are not entitled to receive holiday or sick pay; maternity leave or pay; redundancy pay or notice; an occupational pension; and they cannot bring unfair dismissal charges. Relatively few homeworkers receive a contract or pay slip. Employment status varies between the traditional homeworkers and the 'new' homeworkers – for example, those employed in computer programming and systems analysis. The new homeworkers are more likely to have employee status. The Low Pay Unit found that half of their sample of new homeworkers described themselves as 'self-employed' and that nine out of ten employees were paid for holidays and sickness.[27] This was in marked contrast to the traditional homeworkers in their sample, where none received sick or holiday pay.

To some extent, therefore, the composition of the homework labour force has changed and one of these changes has been the development of homeworking in the area of new technology. Differences based on class, education and skill (and hence earning potential) separate the new from the traditional homeworkers. Whereas traditional homeworkers often do work unrelated to their previous employment, the new homeworkers often perform similar tasks to those they had done as office workers. However, the majority of both groups share the same reason for working at home – the need to combine paid employment with childcare responsibilities.[28]

The other major change in the composition of the homework labour force has been the addition of large numbers of immigrant women. Language difficulties and cultural constraints prevent many of these women from working outside the home. Many immigrant women are recruited from amongst the Cypriot, Bangladeshi, Pakistani, Indian and East African communities. They are concentrated in particular areas such as London's East End, the traditional heartland of sweated labour in the clothing industry. Within the inner city areas, many manufacturing industries are now in decline and as husbands are made redundant, more women seek employment:

As the recession deepened after 1981, clothing factories closed and men lost their jobs – while the supply of work to female Bangladeshi homeworkers increased. Increasingly work is undertaken by the family unit with young children expected to play their part in production.[29]

The ease with which homeworking can be adapted to fit in with cultural constraints and the traditional values of the immigrant families is reminiscent of the adoption of homework by sectors of the working class during the period of economic and social upheaval in the wake of the Industrial Revolution.[30] In both instances homework can be seen as the system of employment which resulted in the least conflict and disruption of the traditional gender roles.

A number of studies have been concerned with the role of the family in adapting workers to new industrial conditions. They have tended to concentrate on a particular immigrant group and its adaptation to the new economic conditions. These studies have sought to understand the role of cultural, economic and demographic conditions and traditions in determining the choice and relationship between work and family for immigrant women.[31] In studying the immigrant's adaptation to a new type of society, 'we are examining a dynamic process, a give and take between new conditions and old social forms'.[32] V. Yans-McLaughlin, in her study of Buffalo Italians found that they chose work-styles and occupational modes which resulted in minimal strain upon traditional family patterns. In the case of the Buffalo Italians homework was a semi-traditional occupation and was therefore a popular choice of employment.

Homework fulfils many similar functions for immigrants in England today. For example, homework appealed to many women in the nineteenth century because it could be kept secret and it still has this appeal today, particularly for many immigrant women and their husbands:

> The women will not discuss their work with anyone . . . They may have financial fears, or they don't want anyone to know because of personal prestige, or their husband feels no one must know his wife is working.[33]

Homeworkers are recruited from the immigrant communities, from amongst those who cannot speak English and from those women whose husbands insist that they do not leave the home.

Needless to say, these women are a particularly vulnerable sector of the population, seldom being aware of their rights and of employment alternatives. Immigrants are generally found concentrated in the lowest-paid and least-skilled jobs in the economy. It is not surprising therefore that immigrant women who suffer a double oppression (sexism and racism) should be found in large numbers in homework, the most sweated labour force of all. Many immigrant women must also take up homework for the same fundamental reasons as English women, that is, the lack of childcare provision.

In looking at the preponderance of immigrants in homework, cultural explanations of their choice of employment should not be overplayed. Many of these women, even when they have learnt to speak English and even when their husbands permit them to work outside the home, will still be forced to resort to homework. The prejudice immigrants meet at the hands of employers must also be seen as an integral part of the explanation of immigrant women's 'choice' of employment in the United Kingdom today.

Homeworkers are not always aware of just how low their earnings are. Many do not actually calculate how much they earn in an hour; others feel that they are lucky to be allowed to work at home and low wages are the price to be paid for this privilege. Many are also aware that if they complain someone else will readily take their place. Although homework is particularly badly paid, it is worth remembering that many of the alternative jobs that homeworkers might apply for also thrive on sweated labour – many of the small clothing factories that employ large numbers of immigrant women pay well below the Statutory Minimum Rate (SMR). The women are employed in dangerous and insanitary working conditions with overcrowding, no heating, no separate washing and toilet facilities, and no provision of canteens or eating places.[34] The new homeworkers fare rather better, especially those with employee status. However, their wages still remain low relative to their counterparts employed in offices. They are also disadvantaged in terms of promotion and training prospects.

Even the low rates of pay do not reveal the real depth of the exploitation of homeworkers, who still receive no compensation for the social and domestic disruption incurred through working at home. Kitchens or living rooms are often piled high with the paraphernalia of homeworking, causing disruption to family life. The entire family is subjected to the hazards and dangers of using the home as a workplace, the house and furnishings may be subject to extra wear and tear and any protective clothing such as overalls or rubber gloves must be bought by the homeworker herself. With the use of inflammable materials such as glue, and with storage of goods resulting in overcrowding, fire is an obvious risk. In 1949 the *Daily Herald* reported the death of a mother, grandmother and three children in a fire after a rubber solution had been accidentally knocked into the fire: the mother had worked at covering shoe heels in the sitting room of her council house in Bristol.[35] The Low Pay Unit uncovered a wide range of health complaints amongst homeworkers. Headaches, eye-strain, backaches, stomach pains, depression, stress and excessive tiredness are commonplace ailments.[36] Although many of the more dangerous trades are now no longer carried out in the home, many health and safety hazards remain.

Homework may even be used to evade the more rigorous safety at work legislation that was passed in the 1970s. For example, the following is an extract from a letter sent to *Woman* magazine in 1979:

> Since the asbestos scare a couple of years ago, stores personnel at the nationalised industry I work for are not obliged to handle anything made of asbestos. So all asbestos parts are collected by an outside contractor and returned individually bagged. Who does the bagging? You've guessed it – homeworkers. It's a very simple job, the children could help.[37]

The employer of homeworkers continues to be relieved of the cost of basic overheads of rates, rent, heating and lighting: he still pays only for time spent productively. All the rights that the labour movement has fought for during the last century are denied to the homeworker; she is not paid for tea and lunch breaks and receives neither sick pay nor holiday pay. These are all concealed ways of increasing the rate of exploitation and many homeworkers are themselves unaware of the extent to which they are exploited.

It has been argued that the real benefit of working at home is the freedom to control one's working conditions and work-load: the worker is not tied by a set working day. This freedom is, of course, a myth in the case of homework. The homeworker cannot choose when to work or how much work to do. It is the employer who determines her output by payment on a piece-work basis and by the timing of the supply and collection of work. Her flexibility is also curtailed by domestic considerations. She has most often chosen homework in order to enable her to continue to fulfil her non-waged work in the home and the low wages neccessitate working long hours – many homeworkers must work until late at night or get up especially early in the morning. The flexibility of homework is that it permits the worker to overwork, and to extend her working day well past what is considered reasonable and healthy. Homework is more obtrusive than factory work. There are no set hours but the apparatus of homeworking is a constant reminder of what is still to be done. As she has not been out to work, it is likely that demands from the family make little allowance for time and energy expended on her waged work.

Homework is often acceptable to the rest of the family in a way that a woman going out to work would not be. S. Allen and C. Wolkowitz found that:

> The decision to do homework rather than go out to work is frequently made by the husband. Fifty homeworkers (50 per cent of the sample) said that their families expected them to stay at home rather than go out to work.[38]

Many women also feel a pressure or duty to keep up recognised standards of housework that become an increasing burden with the added feature of homework. The separation of home and workplace at least makes the double workload more evident both to the woman and her family.

Since the Second World War there has been no significant legislation affecting the situation of the homeworker. Responsibility for the health and safety of homeworkers lies with local authorities who are supposed to keep lists, supplied by employers, of all local homeworkers. The 1959 Wages Council Act emphasised that these lists should be kept up to date.[39] However, as in the period before the Second World War, these lists have been shown to be unreliable. This was the view of the Commission on Industrial Relations (CIR) when they carried out their investigation into homework in 1969. A community worker in the East London Borough of Newham said:

> Employers just don't report to the local authority, and the local

authority doesn't encourage or force employers to do this. The public health department is understaffed and homeworkers are very low priorities. The lists in Newham are partial, inaccessible and out of date. And the homeworker has no idea they exist.[40]

The 1961 Factories Act again emphasised that employers should keep lists of all their homeworkers and submit them to the local authority twice-yearly. The CIR found that nearly 70 per cent of the employers interviewed claimed to know nothing about the registration procedure. The continued shortage of wages inspectors also means that a relatively low incidence of employers are caught out. Those homeworkers covered by a wages council should be paid a SMR and employers must produce records to a wages inspector if requested. The inspector, however, does not have the authority to enter a person's home unless invited. The present government's proposed restrictions on wages councils may further weaken their influence on wage rates paid to workers who have no other form of protection.

The 1970s witnessed some attempt to strengthen legislation to protect homeworkers. For example, a Homeworking Unit was established within the Wages Inspectorate. However, during the 1980s central government has lost interest in homeworkers and attempts to improve their position have been conducted on a more local level with, for example, certain councils appointing a Homeworking Officer. But still the home or workplace does not fall under the scope of protective legislation even today – we are forced to conclude that few, if any, advances have been made since the days of the 1901 Factory Act and the 1909 Trade Boards Act.

Trade unions also have made little headway into organising the mass of homeworkers: the overwhelming majority are still not members of any trade union and the problems confronting the trade unions in their attempts to organise homeworkers have changed little since the turn of the century. Indeed, an additional difficulty has been the large influx of immigrants into the homework labour force. Culturally-determined relationships and attitudes often spill over into the work situation:

Relationships of servility, subservience and passivity evident between husband and wife or mother-in-law and daughter-in-law in the home were reproduced to an important extent at work. The relationship between employer and worker was underpinned by the conventional relationship between man and woman in the Asian community.[41]

Cultural factors have further added to the already seemingly insurmountable obstacles in the way of unionising homeworkers. A large number of homeworkers are in the clothing industry, where trade unionism has already been weakened by the decline of large factories. This decline in large-scale production means that production in clothing manufacture is more reminiscent of that of a century ago. Only half of the clothing workforce today belongs to the NUTGW. However, the problem of unionisation does not just relate to homeworkers: it has also proved very difficult to unionise many of the small factories that have come to proliferate within the clothing industry. The reservoir of Asian female labour and homeworkers has helped to weaken the unions' bargaining position.

The movement to organise homeworkers has never regained the momentum it had at the end of the last century. Indeed, it is the feeling of many that the unions have neglected the homeworker. In 1968 the TUC sent out a circular to unions and to the Secretary of State for Employment and Productivity about conditions under which homework was being carried out, and requested an enquiry and stricter control. Also in 1968, the TUC Women's Conference passed a resolution against the banning of homework.[42] In 1971, Ethel Chipchase, secretary of the TUC Women's Advisory Committee, asked Robert Carr, then Secretary of Employment, to initiate a study on the extent and hazards of homeworking:

> It was never done. But women are used to waiting. The first call for equal pay was in 1888. Ever since I came to the TUC around twelve years ago resolutions about homeworking have been coming up at Conference. And, of course, there was concern long before that.[43]

In 1975, following the suggestion of the NUTGW, the TUC asked the Department of Employment to deal with homeworking in the Employment Protection Bill. In particular, they asked that the unions should have the right to see local authority lists, that a new register of homeworkers should be established and that wages councils should award extra allowances to homeworkers to cover the overheads which would be paid by employers in a factory. The Department of Employment stated that wages councils already had the power to award such allowances but did not do so. They claimed that inspections had shown only a small number of homeworkers paid less than the SMR. They also stated that the disclosure of information obtained under the statutory powers would make the task of inspectors more difficult.

Although it may well be correct to criticise unions for their lack of success and commitment to unionising homeworkers, the difficulties they face should not be underestimated. Now, as at the turn of the century, homeworkers are an isolated and scattered work-force and there are still many homeworkers who wish to keep their employment as secret as possible, so the fight to unionise homeworkers is as difficult now as it has ever been. If unionisation is to be the ultimate panacea for ending sweated labour then legislation is needed to pave the way for the trade union movement. Homeworkers have long been resented by factory employees and trade unionists, being seen as undercutting union rates and undermining collective bargaining, but more recently the official attitude of the trade union movement has changed. The TUC now recommends that homeworkers should be encouraged to join unions, not only so that they can gain the benefit of protection but also to ensure that they are not used to undermine the industrial position of the factory workers.

There are, of course, those who feel that the only answer to the problems of homeworking is a total prohibition. In realistic terms this is not an immediate solution – broader social changes would need to precede such action. It only becomes a realistic proposition when the reasons that force so many to take up homework have been eradicated. This means that social security benefits and pensions must ensure an adequate standard of living so that it is not necessary to resort to sweated labour. It also means that it must be possible for those women who need to earn to go out to work. This involves the provision of adequate nursery and childcare facilities. Only when these sorts of reforms have been inaugurated does it even become feasible to talk in terms of the abolition of homework. Meanwhile, a number of proposals have been suggested that could improve the situation of today's homeworkers: a statutory minimum wage is necessary, with a strengthening of the Wages Inspectorate to enforce this; homework rates of pay should be the same as those for on-site workers with a supplement paid to compensate for use of the home as a workplace; homeworkers need to be given employment protection rights, plus the paid holidays, sick pay and maternity leave of other workers; statutory registration of all homeworkers is also recommended, with employers making half-yearly returns to local authorities – it is also suggested that trade unions should have access to these lists; the Health and Safety Commission also need to press for legislation to improve protection for homeworkers; and there is the need to prohibit the use of dangerous equipment and hazardous materials in the home.

Today the composition of the homework labour force is slightly different from that of the nineteenth and early twentieth century but many of the reasons for choosing homework remain basically unchanged. The attractions of homework to certain sectors of the female population have altered relatively little since the nineteenth century. Numbers of women often return to the labour market on completion of their family and after a long period in the home. These women frequently have no particular skill to offer, and their confinement in the domestic sphere has eroded much of their self-confidence. To these women, homework can appear an attractive proposition. In other instances, for example where the woman is the breadwinner of a one-parent family, or where the woman must remain at home to care for a sick or disabled elderly dependant or young children, homework must seem to be the answer. These women, and especially large numbers of immigrant women, the elderly and the disabled make up the bulk of today's homework labour force.

Homework has consistently reinforced the ideology that woman is primarily a domestic creature whose inherent nature makes her best suited to perform the roles of wife and mother and the view that housework and childcare is the sole responsibility of the woman is strengthened by women doing waged work in the home. The fact that the workplace is the home has been and continues to be an absolutely crucial determinant of the status of homework and of the attitude the women have to this form of waged work. It seems that homework is less likely to be seen as 'real' work because the woman does not actually 'go out to work'. As the waged work is fitted in between the demands of the home and family it merges with her domestic work role. The fact that the woman is undertaking a double work load is thus disguised to a greater extent than if, for example, she was a factory worker.

The implications for this sense of false consciousness are grave. It means that the majority of homeworkers will never see themselves as part of a collective labour force and are likely therefore to remain particularly unresponsive to calls for unionisation. Apathy and despondency towards their work situation is heightened by the fact that most homework is of a monotonous and repetitive nature often demanding little or no skill or imagination, while the hours are long, the material rewards low and the job satisfaction negligible. Homework also reinforces a woman's isolation and denies her the companionship of other workers. The absence of unionisation deprives her of an access to politics and the chance to develop an awareness of herself as a working woman with interests outside the home.

The difference in status between indoor work and homework has been underpinned by the much lower wage rates of the latter. The idea of homework as an easy and convenient option is still pushed today and reinforced by advertisements that invite women to 'work in the comfort of your own sitting room'. The discrepancy in earnings between men's and women's wages has always been substantial, and homework has always been thought of as 'women's work'. Certainly, the pittance earned in the sweated homework trades and the unreliability in the supply of work has meant that homework could seldom be said to have provided women with any form of economic independence. Further, as homework does not take women out of the home it does not conflict with their traditional social sphere of activity. Homework thrives upon the fact that women have been trapped in their own homes by the unpaid demands made upon them as housewives and childcarers. Although the composition of the homework labour force has changed since the First World War its predominant characteristic, that of being a female labour force, has remained unaltered.

Only when labour has been scarce have women been encouraged, and enabled, to take up employment across the broad spectrum of the economy. It is still accepted today that women will work for lower wages and with less job security than their male counterparts. Despite the passing of a Sex Discrimination Act and an Equal Pay

Act the average industrial manual wage for women is still only around 60 per cent of the average male wage. Although the TUC has been pledged to equal pay since the 1880s there is a long history of trade unions colluding with management in order to evade their responibilities *vis-à-vis* equal pay and, perhaps most importantly, equal opportunities.

Of course, it is not only the attitudes of men that must change in order to alter the present sexual inequalities, but the expectations and aspirations of women as well. It appears that nothing less than a social revolution is required to change our perception of men's and women's work. As we have seen, the structure of the family and women's social status is inseparable from women's economic status. Far-reaching changes in society are needed to eradicate the problems associated with homework as it exists today. Homework cannot be relegated to history and indeed shows every indication of remaining a good economic proposition for employers for many years to come.

Notes

Chapter 1: A woman's place is in the home

1. H. Land (1980) 'The Family Wage', *Feminist Review* 6, p. 60.
2. L. Oren (1974) 'The Welfare of Women in Labouring Families in England 1860 –1950' in M. Hartmann and L. Banner (eds) *Clio's Conciousness Raised: New Perspectives on the History of Women*, p. 138.
3. See N. J. Smelser (1959) *Social Change in the Industrial Revolution*.
4. A. Davin (1979) 'Mind that you do as you are told: reading books for Board School girls', *Feminist Review* 5, p. 90.
5. E. Gaskell (1885) *North and South*, p.109.
6. I. Pinchbeck (1930) *Women Workers and the Industrial Revolution*, p. 99.
7. Lady F. Bell (1907) *At the Works* (repub. Virago, 1984).
8. Pinchbeck (1930) *Women Workers*, p. 185.
9. N. Osterud (1978) 'Women's work in nineteenth-century Leicester: A Case Study in the Sexual Division of Labour', unpublished paper, now available in A. V. John (ed) (1986) *Unequal Opportunities.Women's Employment in England 1800–1918* (Oxford: Basil Blackwell). This collection also contains other relevant articles relating to women's work.
10. All interview extracts in the book are from interviews carried out by Belinda Westover with women in the Colchester area between 1975 and 1982. All the women had been tailoresses, many of them homeworkers. Several of their mothers and grandmothers had also been homeworker tailoresses. Names have been changed to respect the confidentiality of those interviewed. Most of them had started work just before or during the First World War.
11. Eisenstein (1984) *Give us Bread, But Give Us Roses*, p. 145.
12. Some of the material and ideas contained in this chapter are from L. Davidoff and B. Westover (eds) (1986) *Our Work, Our Lives, Our Words*, (London: Macmillan).

Chapter 2: Homeworkers: work and family life

1. H. Wood (1893) *Mrs Haliburton's Troubles*, p. 97.
2. Ibid., p. 96.

3. J. C. Dony (1842) *A History of the Straw Plait Industry*, p. 110.

4. Parliamentary Papers 1867–8 Royal Commission on Agriculture XV11, p. 195.

5. Parliamentary Papers 1908 Select Committee on Homework, Introduction.

6. Miss Hackness (ed) (1889) *Toilers in London*, p. 238.

7. C. Booth (1891) *Life and Labour of the People in London*, vol. 1. p.445.

8. Ibid.

9. Report of the Outer London Inquiry Committee: West Ham, A Study in Social and Industrial Problems (1907), p. 268.

10. See Chapter 5 in this volume.

11. Parliamentary Papers 1908 Select Committee on Homework, p. 69.

12. West Ham Inquiry (1907), p. 268.

13. Reverend B. Lambert (1868) 'East London Pauperism' (sermon preached before the University of Oxford).

14. A. M. Brigg (1874) 'The Cry against Homework', *Nineteenth Century*, December, p. 974.

Chapter 3: Homework and economic change, 1850 – 1914

1. K. Marx (1869) *Capital*, vol. 1 (New York, 1969 edn) p. 466

2. Ibid., p. 510

3. J. H. Clapham (1964) *An Economic History of Modern Britain*, vol. 1, p. 179.

4. K. Marx (1867) p. 461.

5. See R. Samuel (1977) 'The Workshop of the World: Steampower and Hand Technology in mid-Victorian Britain', *History Workshop Journal*, no. 3 (Spring).

6. D. S. Landes (1968) *The Unbound Prometheus*, p. 10.

7. W. Ashworth (1960) *An Economic History of England 1870 – 1939*, p. 26.

8. See Chapter 5 of this volume.

9. D. Bythell (1978) *The Sweated Trades*, p. 108.

10. See Chapter 4 of this volume for further discussion.

11. B. Taylor (1979) 'The Men are as Bad as their Masters: Socialism, Feminism and Sexual Antagonism in the London Trades in the early 1830s', *Feminist Studies*, Spring, p. 27.

12. G. Stedman Jones (1971) *Outcast London*, p. 107.

13. See A. Fox (1958) *A History of the National Union of Boot and Shoe Operatives 1874 – 1957*, Oxford University Press.

14. See Chapter 7 of this volume for a detailed discussion on legislation.

Chapter 4: Types of homework

1. J. Burnett (1969) *A History of the Cost of Living*, p. 250. The wages of agricultural labourers were higher in the North and North-West of England

than in the South and East where no alternative industrial employment was available. Improvements in their wages did not come about until the 1870s. Burnett estimates the average wage of the agricultural labourer as 11s. 7d. a week in 1860 and 13s. in 1866, but the Select Committee Report on the Rate of Agricultural Wages showed that wages could be as little as 3s. a week in the South for a single man and 4s. 6d. for a married man.

2. See G. Stedman Jones (1971) *Outcast London*.

3. See Chapter 5 in this volume.

4. Select Committee of the House of Lords on the Sweating System (1888–90).

5. Royal Commission on Labour (1893–4) pt. 1, XXXVII, vol 5, p. 623.

6. See J. A. Schmiechen (1975) 'Sweated Industries and Sweated Labour: A Study of Industrial Disorganisation and Worker Attitudes in the London Clothing Trades 1867–1909', University of Illinois, D. Phil. thesis. Now available as *Sweated Industries and Sweated Labour* (Croom Helm 1984).

7. See also Chapter 5.

8. Royal Commission on Labour (1893–4) Pt. 1, The Employment of Women, vol. V.

9. P. Thompson and T. Vigne, 'Family Life and Work Experience before 1918', project interview at the University of Essex, no. 257.

10. Miss Harkness (ed.) (1889) *Toilers in London*, pp. 54–5.

11. C. Black (ed.) (1915) *Married Women's Work*, p. 30.

12. T. E. Schulz, 'The Woodstock Glove Industry', *Oxoniensa*, 193, 111, p. 149.

13. C. Black (ed.) (1915), *Married Women's Work*, p. 20.

14. P. Thompson and T. Vigne, 'Family Life and Work Experience before 1918'; project interviews, at the University of Essex, No. 198.

15. Children's Employment Commission (1863), 1st rep., XVIII, p. 182.

16. C. Freeman (n.d.) *Pillow Lace in the East Midlands* (Luton Museum and Art Gallery Public).

17. T. Wright (1919) *The Romance of the Lace Pillow* (1971 edn.) p. 156.

18. P. Thompson and T. Vigne, project interviews no. 406.

19. Children's Employment Commission (1863) 1st rep., XVIII, p. 186.

20. A. W. Hopkinson (1903) 'Home Industries in Nottingham', *Economic Review*, July, pp. 336–7.

21. Thompson and Vigne, Project Interviews, no. 217.

22. C. Freeman (n.d.) *Luton and the Hat Industry*, p. 13.

23. H. G. Fitzrandolph (1949) *Rural Industries of East Anglia and Essex* (Essex Record Office 16).

24 *Old People's Essays*, Essex Record Office, T/2 25/75.

25. J. G. Dony (1942) *A History of the Straw Hat Industry*, p. 140.

26. C. Booth (1891) *Life and Labour of the People of London*, vol. 1. p. 431.

27. Women's Industrial Council (1897) *Home Industries of Women in London*, Introduction.

28. Will Thorne, MP (1925) *My Life's Battles*, p. 16.

29. E. Cadbury, M. C. Matheson and G. Shann (1906) *Women's Work and Wages*, pp. 150–8.

30. See R. H. Sherard (1896) 'The White Slaves of England', *Pearson's Magazine*.

31. *Daily News* (1910) Midland edn: 14th September. See Chapter 7 for a discussion of the chain-makers' strike.

Chapter 5: The tailoring industry, 1850–1914

1. J. Scott (1982) 'The Mechanisation of Women's Work', *Scientific American*, September, p. 137.

2. J. R. Long (1949) 'Location Theory and the Clothing Industry' (unpublished PhD thesis, University of Leeds), p. 67.

3. J. Thomas (1955) *A History of the Leeds Clothing Industry*, p. 34.

4. D. Bythell (1978) *The Sweated Trades*, p. 70.

5. R. H. Tawney (1915) *The Establishment of minimum rates in the Tailoring Industry under the Trade Boards Act of 1909*, p. 22.

6. S. Dodds (1928) *The Clothing Workers of Great Britain*, p. 34.

7. B. Potter in C. Booth (1902) *Life and Labour of the People of London*, vol. V, p. 37.

8. See Chapter 6 of this volume.

9. E. Hunt (1973) *Regional Wage Variation in Britain 1850–1914*, p. 313.

10. J. Buckmann (1968) 'The Economic and Social History of Alien Immigrants to Leeds 1880–1914' (unpublished PhD thesis, University of Strathclyde) p. 44.

11. C. Collett in Booth (1902) p. 470.

12. J. Buckmann (1968) p. 128.

13. Much of the empirical research on which this chapter is based was carried out in Colchester. All interview material comes from the Colchester area.

14. Tawney (1915) p. 111.

15. See Chapter 4 in this volume for a discussion of the rural home industries.

16. *Essex County Standard*, 5 October 1912.

17. C. Black (1913) *Married Women's Work*, p. 240.

18. *East Anglian Times*, 13 November 1912.

19. Report of the Select Committee of the House of Lords on the Sweating System (1890) p. 920.

20. A. Brown (1980) *Colchester 1815–1914* p. 25.

21. *Victoria County History of Essex*, p. 484.

22. Interview with Canon Turner, grandson of Thomas Bentley Turner, carried out in 1982.

23. *Essex County Standard*, 4 March 1893.

24. *Essex County Standard*, 4 November 1893.

25. P. Thompson and T. Vigne, 'Family Life and Work Experience before 1918', project interviews at the University of Essex no. 137.

26. See Chapter 7 of this volume.

Chapter 6: Homework as sweated labour

1. C. Booth (1902) *Life and Labour of the People of London* (First series, vol. IV).

2. Ibid., p. 330.

3. Ibid., p. 334.

4. Ibid., p. 342.

5. D. F. Schloss (1890) 'The Sweating System', *Fortnightly Review*.

6. Select Committee of the House of Lords on the Sweating System (1888) 1st rep. vol. 20, p. 319.

7. E. Halevy, *A History of the English People in the Nineteenth Century*, vol. 6, *The Rule of Democracy 1905–1914* (1934), p. 247.

8. Ibid., p. 242.

9. Select Committee of the House of Lords on the Sweating System (1890) p. 258.

10. Ibid., p. 207.

11. B. Hutchins (1926) *A History of Factory Legislation*, p. 215.

12. Ibid., p. 219.

13. C. Black (1907) *Sweated Industry and the Minimum Wage*, p. 2.

14. Select Committee on Homework (1908) p. 3.

15. D. F. Schloss, *Methods of Industrial Remuneration* (1892) pp. 5–6.

16. *Women's Trade Union Review* (1896) October, p. 16.

17. 'High Ideals: Early Married Life. A Paper for Working Women', *The Girl's Own Paper* (1895) vol. XV, February 2, p. 275.

18. Clara Collett in C. Booth (1891) *Life and Labour of the People of London*, vol. 1 p. 450.

19. R. H. Tawney (1915) *The Establishment of Minimum Rates in the Tailoring Industry under the Trade Boards Act of 1909*, p. 192.

20. R. Mudie Smith, (1906) *Sweated Industries: A Handbook of the Daily News Exhibition*, May, p. 36.

21. *Royal Commission on the Housing on the Working Classes* (1884–5) vol. XXI, p. 170.

22. H. Bosenquet (1902) 'A Study in Women's Wages', *Economic Journal*, March, p. 44.

23. Royal Commission on the Housing of the Working Classes (1884–5) vol. XXI, p. 221.

24. B. P. Thompson and E. Yeo (eds) *The Unknown Mayhew* (1973) p. 177.

25. See, for example, W. J. Walker's statement, Director of the Working Women's Co-operative Association, *Select Committee on the Sweating System* (1889), 4th rep. vol. 14, p. 444.

26. E. H. Hunt (1973) *Regional Wage Variations in Britain 1850–1914*, Oxford.

27. C. Black (1915) *Married Women's Work*, p. 43.

28. S. Webb and A. Freeman (1912) *Seasonal Trades*, p. 46.

29. Report of Outer London Inquiry Committee, *West Ham: A study in Social and Industrial problems* (1907) p. 261.

30. I. O. Ford (n.d.) 'Women's Wages and the Conditions under which they are Earned' in H. S. Salt (ed.) *Cruelties of Civilisation*.

31. M. Irwin (1907) *The Problem of Homework* p. 10.

32. Report of the Outer London Inquiry Committee, *West Ham: A study in Social and Industrial Problems* (1907) p. 273.

33. C. Meyer and C. Black (1909) *Makers of our Clothes*, p. 65.

34. J. A. Hobson (1891) *Problems of Poverty*, p. 156.

35. *Royal Commission on the Housing of the Working Classes* (1884–5) vol. XXXI, p. 18.

36. Ibid., vol. XXX, p. 18.

37. *Select Committee on Homework* (1908) pp. 1821–2.

38. Report of the Outer London Inquiry Committee, *West Ham: A study in Social and Industrial Problems* (1907) p. 260.

39. E. F. Hogg (1897) 'The Fur-Pullers of South London', *Nineteenth Century*, November p. 735.

40. R. Cross (1882) 'Homes of the Poor in London', *Nineteenth Century*, p. 239.

41. P. Thompson and T. Vigne, 'Family Life and Work Experience before 1918', project interviews, University of Essex, no. 257.

42. C. Kingsley (Parson Lot) (1889) 'Cheap Clothes and Nasty', *Alton Locke*, p. XIX.

43. Miss Harkness (ed.) (1889) *Toilers in London*, p. 52.

44. A. H. Brigg (1894) 'The Cry Against Homework', *Nineteenth Century*, December, p. 975.

45. Quoted by Mrs McLaren (1890) *The Sweating System, A Summary of the evidence given before the House of Lords with comments and suggestions*.

46. B. L. Hutchins (1907) 'Homeworking and Sweating', Fabian Tract no. 130.

Chapter 7: Legislation and trade unions

1. B. S. Nowell-Smith (ed.) (1964) *Edwardian England* p. 56.

2. Ibid., p. 62.

3. Gained in 1867 and 1884.

4. B. Gilbert (1973) *The Evolution of the Welfare State*, p. 13.

5. Ibid., p. 26.

6. Ibid., p. 60.

7. H. Emy (1973) *Liberals, Radicals and Social Politics 1892–1914*, p. 30.

8. B. Webb and S. Webb (1897) *Industrial Democracy*, p. 775.

9. Ibid., p. 783.

10. See *Daily News*, 12 June 1907 and 24 September 1906; *Manchester Weekly Times*, 22 September 1906.

11. Mrs J. R. Macdonald (1908) 'The development and present condition of homework in relation to the legal protection of workers' in Women's Industrial Council, *Home Industries of Women in London*.

12. *Select Committee on Homework* (1908), p. vii.

13. W. H. Wilkins (1893) 'The Bitter Cry of the Voteless Toilers' (Women's Emancipation Union).

14. E. G. Howarth and M. Wilan (1907)'West Ham: A Study in Social and Industrial Problems', *Report of the Outer London Inquiry Committee*.

15. *Select Committee on Homework* (1908).

16. *Daily News*, 26 March, 1908.

17. London Women's Industrial Council (1906) *Bill for the Better Regulation of Homework*.

18. B. H. Hutchins (1907) 'Homework and Sweating', Fabian Tract no. 130.

19. V. de Vesselitsky (1916) *The Homeworker and her Outlook*, p. 295.

20. D. Sells (1923) *The British Trade Boards System* (Washington) p. 53.

21. R. H. Tawney (1915) *The Establishment of Minimum Rates in the Tailoring Industry under the Trade Boards Act of 1909*, p. 184.

22. Ibid., p. 205.

23. H. D. Roberts (1912) *The Tragedy of the Woman Worker* (Liverpool Anti-sweating League).

24. *Select Committee on Homework* (1907) minutes and evidence, p. 137.

25. See Chapter 9 for continuing discussion on legislation and homework.

26. Except in the late 1880s and 1890s when unions of unskilled workers had considerable success.

27. M. Hamilton (1941) *Women at Work*, p. 12.

28. R. Strachey (1928) *The Cause*, p. 238.

29. M. Hamilton (1941) *Women at Work*, p. 15.

30. J. Bornat (1977)'Home and Work: A New Context for Trade Union History', *Oral History*, vol. V, no. 2 (Autumn), p. 63.

31. Ibid.

32. B. Drake (1921) *Women in Trade Unions*, p. 199.

33. C. Coates (1982) 'Opening the Cage Door', *Spare Rib*, no. 121 (August) p. 50.

34. Ibid., p. 51.

35. Lady Dilke (1892) 'Trade Unions for Women', *North American Review*, p. 3.

36. Trade Union Congress (1955) *Women in the Trade Union Movement*.

37. *Select Committee on Homework* (1907) minutes and evidence, p. 121.

38. Ibid., p. 122.

39. Ibid., p. 134.

40. A. Bulley and M. Whitely (1894) *Women's Work*, p. 87.

41. C. Black (1907) *Sweated Industry and the Minimum Wage*.

42. *Select Committee on the Sweating System* (1890) 5th rep. vol. 17, pp. iii–xiv.

43. C. Booth (1891) *Life and Labour of the People of London*, vol. I, p. 457.

44. *The Woman Worker*, 20 June 1908, p. 97.
45. C. Black (1915) *Married Women's Work* p. 103.
46. *Women's Protective and Provident League*, 16th Annual Report (July 1890), p. 10.
47. *The Morning Post* (18 July 1907).
48. *The Woman Worker*, 20 June 1908, p. 97.
49. *Christian Commonwealth* (19 March 1914).
50. *Select Committee on Homework* (1908).
51. E. Cadbury, M. C. Matheson and G. Shann (1906) *Women's Work and Wages*, p. 250.
52. J. Mallon (1913) 'Trade Boards and Organisation', *Women's Trade Union Review*, no. 88 (January), p. 12.
53. Ibid.
54. Ibid., p. 14.
55. Quoted in 'The Strike of Women Chainmakers, 1910', BBC TV, 23 April 1977.
56. M. MacArthur (1910) 'Slaves of the Forge', *The Christian Commonwealth*, vol. xxx, no. 1508, 7 September.
57. *Birmingham Dispatch*, 1 September 1910.
58. Gertrude Tuckwell Collection, TUC Library.
59. Quoted in 'The Strike of Women Chainmakers, 1910, BBC TV, 23 April 1977.

Chapter 8: Homework 1914–1945

1. A. Marwick (1977) *Women at War, 1914–18*, p. 37.
2. D. Mitchell (1966) *Women on the Warpath*, p. 33.
3. Marwick (1977) pp. 73–4.
4. Standing Joint Committee of Industrial Women's Organisation (n.d.) *The Position of Women After the War*.
5. Increased Employment of Women during the War in the U.K., Dep., p. 16, 1919.
6. Quoted in Mitchell (1966) pp. 250–1.
7. P. Thompson and T. Vigne, 'Family Life and Work Experience before 1918', project interviews at the University of Essex, no. 51.
8. Women's Advisory Committee, Rep. 1919, p. 36.
9. Marwick (1977) p. 16.
10. *The Women's Dreadnought*, 20 June 1914.
11. Ibid., 24 October 1914.
12. Ibid., 22 August 1914.
13. Ibid., 24 October 1914.
14. Ibid., 15 May 1915.
15. Ibid., same date.
16. Ibid., 12 December 1914.
17. *Women in the Trade Union Movement*, Report of the Trades Union Congress (1955).
18. Quoted in Mitchell (1966) p. 266.

19. M. Weir (1970) *Shoes were for Sunday*, p. 128.
20. C. L. Mowat (1955) *Britain Between the Wars, 1918–40*, p. 226.
21. Sir H. Llewellyn Smith (ed.) (1930) *The New Survey of London Life and Labour*, vol. I.
22. Ibid., p. 7.
23. Llewellyn Smith (1931) vol. II, p. 1.
24. Ibid., p. 19.
25. Ibid., p. 251.
26. Ibid., p. 254.
27. B. Turner (1927) 'Women in the Labour Market', *The Communist*, vol. 2, no. 10, November, p. 224.
28. N. Branson and M. Heineman (1973) *Britain in the 1930s*, p. 32.
29. Supply of Female Domestic Servants, Committee Reports p.53. Non-Parliamentary Ministry of Labour appointed 1923. Ford, P. and Ford C., *A Breviate of Parliamentary Papers*.
30. Between 1921 and 1931 the numbers of women employed in domestic service went up by 20 000.
31. Llewellyn Smith (1933) Vol. V, p. 139.
32. By 1931 there were 20 000 women in the age group 35–45 registered as charwomen and 19 000 in the 45–55 age group and these official figures underestimate the real numbers. (Census Tables, G.B., 1931.)
33. Llewellyn Smith (1931) vol. II, p. 275.
34. Ibid., p. 259.
35. Ibid., p. 297.
36. Ibid., p. 308.
37. Ibid., p. 309.
38. Ibid., p. 335.
39. Ibid., p. 19.
40. Ibid., p. 24.
41. Ibid., p. 19.
42. Quoted in V. de Vesselitsky (1916) *The Homeworker and her Outlook*, p. 61.
43. Annual Report of Chief Inspector of Factories and Workshops, 1925.
44. Quoted in *The Daily Herald*, 5 February 1924.
45. M. Allen (1979) *A Woman's Place and World War II*, MA thesis, University of Essex.
46. Ibid., p. 120.

Chapter 9: Homework 1945–1985

1. R. Davies (1975) *Women and Work*, p. 71.
2. Figures taken from H. Wainwright (1978) 'Women and the Division of Labour' in P. Abrams (ed.) *Work Urbanisation and Inequality*, p. 115.
3. L. Mackie and P. Patullo (1977) 'Women at Work', p. 40.
4. Davies (1975) p. 20.
5. Mackie and Patullo (1977) p. 74.

6. Davies (1975) p. 18.

7. V. Beechey (1977) 'Some Notes on Female Wage Labour in Capitalist Production', *Capital and Class*, no. 3.

8. Social Trends 16, 1974.

9. A. Coote and B. Campbell (1982) *Sweet Freedom: The Struggle for Women's Liberation*, p. 51.

10. Ibid., p. 52.

11. Ibid., p. 71.

12. *Manchester Guardian*, 'Outwork in the Boot Industry', 7 August 1948.

13. Ibid.

14. *Manchester Guardian*, 'Home Shoemakers too Busy!', 27 October 1953.

15. *The Times*, 'Criticism of Homeworking on Clothing?', 20 September 1953.

16. *Manchester Guardian*, 'Clothing Trade Homework – Call for Enquiry?', 18 June 1957.

17. These include: M. Brown (1974) *Sweated Labour. A Study of Homework* (Low Pay Unit). E. Hope *et al.* (1976) 'Homeworkers in North London' in D. Barker and S. Allen (eds) *Dependence and Exploitation in Work and Marriage*.

18. National Union of Hosiery and Knitwear Workers quoted in *Homeworking: A T.U.C. Statement*, p. 6. (1983).

19. London Industrial Strategy: *The Clothing Industry* (G.L.C) (1985)

20. C. Hakin (1985) *The Employers' Use of Outwork* Department of Employment Research Paper no. 44, April).

21. *Rags to Rags: Low Pay in the Clothing Industry*, Low Pay Unit no. 20 (1982) p. 27.

22. London Industrial Strategy (1985) p. 13.

23. A. Coyle (1984) 'Sex and Skin', p. 23.

24. Ibid., p. 25.

25. Hakin, p. 16.

26. Leicester Outwork Campaign (1983) quoted in L. Bisset and U. Huns: *Sweated Labour: Homeworking in Britain*, Low Pay Unit, no. 198, p. 5.

27. Ibid., p. 25.

28. Ibid., p. 22.

29. *Homeworking: A T.U.C. Statement* (1983) pp. 7–8.

30. See S. Shah (n.d.) *Immigration and Employment in the Clothing Industry*.

31. See V. Yans-McLaughlin (1974) 'A Flexible Tradition', *Journal of Social History*, also T. K. Hareven (1975) 'Family Time and Industrial Time', *Journal of Urban History*, vol. 1, no. 3, May.

32. Yans-McLaughlin (1974) p. 430.

33. Ahmed Din (leader of the Pakistan Association of Newham) quoted in *The Observer Magazine*, 11 July 1976, p. 26.

34. Ibid., p. 37.

35. *Daily Herald*, 26 August 1949.

36. Bisset and Huns (1983) p. 31.

37. *Woman*, 6 October 1979.

38. S. Allen and C. Walkowitz (1986) 'The Control of Women's Labour: The Case of Homeworking', *Feminist Review*, no. 22, February, p. 41.

39. Wages Councils were successors to the Trade Boards (Workers Councils Acts 1945 and 1959). Each Council consists of not more that 3 independent members and equal numbers of employers and workers in the trade or branch of trade concerned. Homeworkers are often unaware of these Councils and therefore cannot actively participate.

40. Quoted in *The Observer Magazine*, 11 July 1976.

41. B. Hoel (n.d.) *Contemporary Clothing 'Sweatshops', Asian Female Labour and Corrective Organisation*, p. 89.

42 B. Bolton (1975) *An End to Homeworking*, Fabian Trust no. 436, p. 8.

43. *Guardian*, January 1975.

Select Bibliography

Place of publication is London unless stated otherwise.

For a detailed bibliography see:

Shelley L. Pennington (1980) 'Women as Homeworkers: An Analysis of the Homework Labour Force in England from 1850 until 1975', Unpublished PhD thesis, University of Essex.

Belinda Westover (1984) 'The Sexual Division of Labour in the Tailoring Industry 1860–1920', Unpublished PhD thesis, University of Essex.

M. Allen (1979) 'Woman's Place and World War II', MA thesis, University of Essex.

S. Allen and C. Walkowitz (1986) 'The Control of Women's Labour: The case of Homeworking': *Feminist Review*, 22 February.

S. Allen and C. Walkowitz (1987) *Homeworking: Myths and Realities.* .

Lady F. Bell (1907) *At the Works*.

C. Black (ed.) (1915) *Married Women's Work*.

C. Black (1907) *Sweated Industry and the Minimum Wage*.

B. Bolton (1975) *An End to Homeworking?* Fabian Tract 436.

C. Booth (1891) *Life and Labour of the People of London*, vol. I.

N. Branson and M. Heineman (1973) *Britain in the Nineteen Thirties*.

G. Braybon (1981) *Women Workers in the First World War*.

A. H. Brigg (1874) 'The Cry Against Homework', *Nineteenth Century*, December.

M. Brown (1974) *A Study of Homework*, Low Pay pamphlet 1, December.

A. Bulley and M. Whitley (1984) *Women's Work*.

D. Bythell (1978) *The Sweated Trades*.

E. Cadbury, M. C. Matheson and G. Shann (1906) *Women's Work and Wages*.

B. Drake (1921) *Women in Trade Unions*.

B. Gilbert (1973) *The Evolution of the Welfare State*.

D. Gittins (1982) *Fair Sex: Family Size and Structure 1900–1939*.

M. Hamilton (1941) *Women at Work*.

E. G. Howarth and M. Wilson (1907) 'West Ham: A Study in Social and Industrial Problems', Report of the Outer London Inquiry Committee.

B. L. Hutchins (1911) *The Working Life of Women*, Fabian Tract 157.

B. L. Hutchins (1907) *Homework and Sweating: The Causes and Remedies*, Fabian Tract 130.

M. Irwin (1907) *The Problems of Homework*.

A. V. John (ed.) (1986) *Unequal Opportunities: Women's Employment in England 1800–1918* (Oxford).

H. Land (1980) 'The Family Wage', *Feminist Review*, 6.

D. S. Landes (1968) *The Unbound Prometheus*.

J. Lewis (ed.) (1986) *Women's Experience of Home and Family, 1850–1940* (Oxford).

L. Mackie and P. Pattullo (1977) *Women at Work*.

E. Mappen (1985) *Helping Women at Work: The Women's Industrial Council 1889–1914*.

A. Marwick (1977) *Women at War 1914–18*.

C. Meyer and C. Black (1909) *Makers of Our Clothes: A Case for Trade Boards*.

D. Mitchell (1966) *Women on the Warpath*.

C. L. Mowat (1955) *Britain Between the Wars 1918–40*.

A. Philips and B. Taylor (1980) 'Sex and Skill: Notes towards a Feminist Economics', *Feminist Review*, 6.

I. Pinchbeck (1930) *Women Workers and the Industrial Revolution 1750–1850*.

M. Spring Rice (1939) *Working Class Wives*.

E. Roberts (1984) *A Woman's Place: An Oral History of Working Class Women 1890–1940*, Oxford.

R. Samuel (1977) 'The Workshop of the World: Steampower and Hand Technology in Mid Victorian Britain', *History Workshop Journal*, 3, Spring.

N. J. Smelser (1959) *Social Change in the Industrial Revolution*.

Sir H. Llewellyn Smith (ed.) (1930–3) *The New Survey of London Life and Labour*, I–V.

R. Mudie Smith (1906) *Sweated Industries. A Handbook of the Daily News Exhibition*.

R. H. Tawney (1914) *The Establishment of Minimum Rates in the Chain-Making Industry under the Trade Boards Act of 1909*.

R. H. Tawney (1915) *The Establishment of Minimum Rates in the Tailoring Industry under the Trade Boards Act of 1909*.

S. Webb and A. Freeman (1912) *Seasonal Trades*.

Women's Industrial Council (1906) *How to Deal with Homework*.

Women's Industrial Council (1906) *Bill for the Better Regulation of Homework*.

Women's Industrial Council (1908) *Home Industries of Women in London*.

Index

Numerals in *italics* refer to captions.